Liv

Muslim Expressions of Faith

Ali S. Asani

I.B.TAURIS

LONDON • NEW YORK • OXFORD • NEW DELHI • SYDNEY

In association with
THE INSTITUTE OF ISMAILI STUDIES
LONDON, 2025

I.B. TAURIS

Bloomsbury Publishing Plc, 50 Bedford Square, London, WC1B 3DP, UK
Bloomsbury Publishing Inc, 1359 Broadway, New York, NY 10018, USA
Bloomsbury Publishing Ireland, 29 Earlsfort Terrace, Dublin 2, D02 AY28, Ireland

BLOOMSBURY, I.B. TAURIS and the I.B. Tauris logo are trademarks
of Bloomsbury Publishing Plc

In association with The Institute of Ismaili Studies
Aga Khan Centre, 10 Handyside Street, London N1C 4DN
www.iis.ac.uk

First published in Great Britain 2025

Copyright © Islamic Publications Ltd, 2025

Ali S. Asani has asserted his right under the Copyright, Designs and
Patents Act, 1988, to be identified as Author of this work.

Series design by www.ianrossdesigner.com

All rights reserved. No part of this publication may be: i) reproduced or
transmitted in any form, electronic or mechanical, including photocopying,
recording or by means of any information storage or retrieval system without
prior permission in writing from the publishers; or ii) used or reproduced in
any way for the training, development or operation of artificial intelligence
(AI) technologies, including generative AI technologies. The rights holders
expressly reserve this publication from the text and data mining exception as
per Article 4(3) of the Digital Single Market Directive (EU) 2019/790.

Bloomsbury Publishing Plc does not have any control over, or responsibility
for, any third-party websites referred to or in this book. All internet
addresses given in this book were correct at the time of going to press.
The author and publisher regret any inconvenience caused if addresses
have changed or sites have ceased to exist, but can accept no
responsibility for any such changes.

A catalogue record for this book is available from the British Library.

A catalog record for this book is available from the Library of Congress.

ISBN: PB: 978-0-7556-5886-2
       ePDF: 978-0-7556-5888-6
       eBook: 978-0-7556-5887-9

Series: World of Islam

Typeset by RefineCatch Limited, Bungay, Suffolk
Printed and bound in Great Britain

For product safety related questions contact productsafety@bloomsbury.com.

To find out more about our authors and books visit
www.bloomsbury.com and sign up for our newsletters.

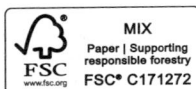

MIX
Paper | Supporting
responsible forestry
FSC
www.fsc.org   FSC® C171272

Contents

Note on the Text

In the interest of readability, diacritics for transliterated words have been limited to the *ayn* (ʿ) and the *hamza* (ʾ) where they occur in the middle of a word. All dates are Common Era, unless otherwise indicated. The word *ibn* 'son of' is abbreviated to *b.* when occurring in the middle of a name, and *bint* 'daughter of' has been abbreviated to *bt.* Unless otherwise specified, English quotations from the Quran are based on the translations of the author.

Introduction

How Do You Know What You Know About Islam?

It has often been said that our world has become a global village. As a result of advances in technology, communication, and travel, people from different religious, cultural, racial, and ethnic backgrounds are in closer contact with each other than at any other time in history. Even so, it is one of the great ironies of our time that this contact has not always resulted in better understanding and appreciation for difference. Rather, our world is marked with great misunderstandings and polarizations, resulting in ever-escalating levels of tension between peoples, cultures, and nations. Alarmed by a perceived threat posed to their identities and values, some have retreated to narrowly constructed racial, tribal, and nationalistic identities. As they increasingly live their lives within smaller and narrower physical and virtual communities, they often define themselves against the 'other'. In some contexts, this binary worldview has been perceived as symptomatic of a clash of civilizations between 'the West' and 'Islam'.

The perspective of the binary between the West and Islam is evident in the thought of some

Figure 1. The London Central Mosque and the Regent's Park Boating Lake
The mosque and the park form a microcosm of the symbolic 'global village'.

contemporary Muslim thinkers as well. Some of these thinkers react to the prevalence of Western influences on many Muslim societies by invoking Islam as a 'political boundary term'[1] and employing 'Islamic' symbols, expressed, for example, through the wearing of specific forms of dress, to assert an identity that is distinctly non-Western.[2] Another group of these thinkers who maintain the existence of the binary nonetheless challenge the usefulness of the categories 'the West' and 'Islam'. They argue that the categories assume that Western and Muslim societies are monolithic, whereas in reality they are marked by immense racial, religious, and ethnic diversity, not to mention diversity of thought and opinions. Their kind of binary categorization, while being more appealing to many, is still flawed from several perspectives. For example, it is historically inaccurate to talk about Western and Islamic civilizations entirely in antagonistic terms when both share common roots in religious ideas and concepts derived from Judaism and Christianity, as well as from Greco-Roman culture.[3] Moreover, such dichotomies are particularly problematic since they are based on humiliating stereotypes of the 'other' and the mistaken assumption that Muslims and non-Muslims cannot possibly hold common ethical and moral values. Hence, some of the opponents of the 'clash of civilizations' perspective argue that we are witnessing what has been described as 'the clash of ignorances' –

Figure 2. His Highness, Aga Khan IV
The late Aga Khan speaking in Ottawa, Canada, in 2006 on the occasion of the signing of the funding agreement for the Global Centre for Pluralism.

a clash that perpetuates fear and hatred of peoples supposedly different from oneself. The late Aga Khan IV expressed a similar sentiment in one of his speeches:

> Those who talk about an inevitable 'clash of civilizations' can point today to an accumulating array of symptoms which sometimes seems to reflect their diagnosis. I believe, however, that this diagnosis is wrong – that its symptoms are more dramatic than they are representative – and that these symptoms are rooted in human ignorance rather than human character.[4]

A key reason for this collective ignorance is religious illiteracy. Without adequate tools and opportunities to understand and engage with religious difference, people tend to represent those who are different from themselves through simplistic caricatures, painting them with a single colour and a single brush stroke, thus stripping them of their humanity. In this sense, the ignorance that is associated with religious illiteracy is not inconsequential; it has serious implications for the multicultural, multiracial, multiethnic, and multireligious world in which we live. The fear, prejudice, and bigotry that it fuels against those who are religiously different tear apart the fabric of society, resulting in violence and instability. Religious illiteracy can also provide the perfect breeding ground for fanaticism. Believers who are ignorant of the complex and diverse ways in which their traditions have developed, both historically and theologically, can easily be swayed by demagogues to adopt narrow and intolerant perspectives. In these ways, religious illiteracy can foster a climate that is 'both politically dangerous and intellectually debilitating'.[5]

What are the characteristics of religious illiteracy? Most common is the tendency to conceptualize religion exclusively in terms of devotional practices such as rites, rituals, and religious festivals. Another is the propensity to attribute the actions of individuals, communities, and nations to their religion. With regard to understanding Islam and Muslim cultures, this latter tendency leads to the assumption among non-Muslims that the faith itself is responsible for everything Muslims do and that whatever happens in a predominantly Muslim country can be attributed to Islam. Thus, many people commonly assume that Islam is the principal cause of a variety of ills that plague some Muslim-majority countries, such as the lack of democracy, economic under-development, and the unjust treatment and marginalization of women. The late Benazir Bhutto, Pakistan's first female prime minister, succinctly summarized this point during a speech entitled 'The Egalitarian Quran vs. Anti-Feminist Interpretations', which she delivered in 1985. She declared: 'It is not Islam which restricts women. It is not Islam which provides for discrimination. It is men.'[6]

Religious illiteracy hinders the ability to look for more complex and more plausible explanations grounded in the understanding that religious traditions and their interpretations are deeply embedded in and shaped by cultural, political, economic, historical, and sociological conditions. It also hampers people from realizing that while a person may invoke religion to legitimize their actions, the primary contexts and motivating forces for their interpretations are often rooted elsewhere. In short, by reducing people's identity to simply their faith, religious illiteracy strips peoples and nations of their humanity, that is, of all that makes them human – their histories, their cultures, their values, their politics, and their social and economic realities.

History is full of examples of conflicts and tragedies that result from a group of people of one religious, racial, or ethnic background failing to accept and respect the humanity of others. The Holocaust, the genocides in Bosnia, Rwanda, and Sudan, the troubles in Northern Ireland, the conflict in Israel and Palestine, and the violence against religious minorities around the world are some recent examples of the consequences of such failures. During times of heightened political and military conflicts, religious illiteracy strongly influences how peoples of different nations, cultures, and religions perceive one another. Frequently, such conflicts employ the language of hyperbole, absolute opposition, and dehumanization – that is, to make a division between the civilized and the barbaric, between good and evil, between us and them. Historically, such stereo-typical perceptions have been common between peoples of the Middle East (Arabs, Persians, and Turks) and Europe and the United States. They are the result of centuries of hostile and confront-ational relationships based on the need for political power and control of economic resources (particularly oil, in recent years) and are couched in the language of conquest and reconquest, *jihad* and crusade, colonialism and nationalism, occu-pation and liberation. In the context of war and armed conflict, such stereotypes often lead to tragic consequences.

Crucial to the construction of knowledge about other peoples and other cultures are our sources of information. Whenever I am invited to talk about Islam, I often begin by asking audiences the questions, 'How do you know what you know about Islam?' and 'What are your sources of information?' We live in a world today in which the media – particularly social media – plays a powerful and historically unprecedented role in shaping what we think we know about our world and in influencing our images of Islam and Muslims. The importance of interrogating our sources of information, as well as the tools we use to construct knowledge based on them, is illus-trated by a well-known story told with slight variations by several authors, including the famous 13th-century Muslim Persian mystic Rumi (d. 1273). Rumi tells a widely-known story about some blind men who attempted to describe an elephant. Each man's perception of the elephant

was limited to his sense of touch as well as his
location vis-à-vis the elephant, which is to say the
specific part of the elephant he touched. For the
person who touched the leg, the elephant was like
a tree; for the one who touched the trunk, it was
like a pipe; while for the one who touched the tail,
it was like a rope. Since none of the blind men had
the ability to see the complete animal, they failed
to appreciate it in its entirety. One can easily
imagine the arguments they would have had over
the shape of the elephant. Similarly, a person's
description of Islam, whether one is Muslim or
not, is based on their 'location or situatedness',
that is, what they have subjectively experienced,
perceived, read, or been taught. People may hold
strikingly contradictory conceptions of Islam
depending on their point of view. For some, Islam
is a religion of peace, while for others it is a political ideology that promotes violence; for some, it
is a religion that oppresses women, for others it is
a religion that promotes equal rights. Many believe
its teachings are compatible with democracy and
fundamental human rights, while others associate
them with dictatorship and tyranny.

Understanding Islam through the
Cultural Studies Approach

So how can we move beyond combative and
ill-informed characterizations of Islam? How is
one to understand the starkly contrasting claims
made in the name of a religion? In a highly polarized world characterized by misinformation, is
it possible to describe Islam – or any religion –

in a manner not coloured by the subjectivity of perception? To assist in responding to such questions and to understand the complex nature of religion, I employ in this book the cultural studies approach. As described in Diane Moore's *Overcoming Religious Illiteracy*, the cultural studies approach stresses the importance of relating understandings and interpretations of religions to the various human contexts in which they are situated. It is based on the premise that religion is a phenomenon embedded in every dimension of human experience. Religions are shaped by a complex web of inextricably linked factors, including political ideologies, socioeconomic conditions, societal attitudes to gender, educational status, literary and artistic traditions, and historical and geographical situations. All of these influence the ways in which religious traditions and their sacred texts, rituals, and practices are interpreted. The complex sociocultural forces that shape religion can, therefore, only be truly understood by utilizing multiple lenses for its study.[7] The cultural studies approach emphasizes a holistic assessment of how these various lenses create a complex picture, and it challenges the assumption that religion can be accurately analysed through a siloed perspective of individual disciplinary lenses.[8] It is a framework through which we can deepen our understanding of religious traditions, by recognizing that they are internally diverse and constantly in flux. Some of these factors may be specific to a local context, or they may be transnational or global in nature.

As these contexts change, the interpretations and characterizations of a tradition also change.

The emphasis that the cultural studies approach places on understanding religion within its multiple contexts is not meant to discredit the study of doctrines, rituals, and scriptures that have come to be identified with various religious traditions. Rather, it serves to deepen literacy about these traditions by orienting the study of them towards the multiplicities of their human context.

For example, many people regard the scriptures and sacred writings as the authoritative embodiments of a religious tradition. They feel that a religion is best understood by reading its scriptures which are perceived as containing its 'true' ethos, or essence. For example, in the aftermath of 9/11, as many sought to understand the possible influence of Islamic teachings on the heinous actions of the terrorists, they turned to the Quran. The underlying assumption was that, in order to acquire a proper understanding of Islam, it was sufficient for a person to read the Quran from cover to cover.

According to the cultural studies approach, granting absolute sovereignty to the text ignores a crucial fact: religious scriptures do not have meaning in and of themselves; they are only given meaning by believers who venerate them and consider them authoritative. Without communities of believers, scriptures are of little significance. In their interpretations, believers are influenced by the historical, political, economic, and cultural contexts in which they live. Since these contexts are dynamic, interpretations of scriptural texts are continually changing as well. Some groups have cited Quranic verses to justify violence in their quest for political hegemony, such as al-Qaeda and ISIS in Afghanistan, Iraq, and Syria, while other Muslims do the opposite. Dekha Ibrahim Abdi, named in 2005 as Kenyan Peace Builder of the Year, draws on verses from the Quran to provide a religious and spiritual base for peace-making and for the arbitration of conflicts between religious and ethnic communities in her country.[9]

The cultural studies approach proposes that it is only by paying close attention to the contexts of interpreters that we can better understand how

Figure 3. Dekha Ibrahim Abdi
Here, Dekha Ibrahim Abdi is being awarded the Hessian Peace Prize 2009 for her commitment to conflict resolution in countries around the world that are divided by religious and ethnic rivalries.

a religious tradition can be depicted and practised in contradictory ways, or how religious
texts, such as the Quran or the Bible, may be
interpreted to justify a wide range of contradictory goals – tolerance and intolerance, liberation
and oppression, democracy and theocracy.

Key to fostering religious literacy through the
cultural studies approach is the realization that
even the way we think about and use the term
'religion' in the 21st century is itself a cultural
construction. The late Wilfred Cantwell Smith,
one of the 20th century's most influential scholars of religion, contends in his book *The Meaning
and End of Religion* that the manner in which
we commonly conceive of religions as homogeneous, systemized ideologies, each with a
distinctive set of scriptures, beliefs, and practices, is a product of the European Enlightenment.
This conception, which is almost universal
today, was disseminated globally when
European powers colonized large parts of the
world, particularly Africa and Asia, from the
19th century onwards. In the process of coloniz-
ing their non-European subjects, Europeans
categorized them on the basis of their practices
and doctrines into 'religions' following European
Christian paradigms. They then proceeded to
label these 'religions' as Mohammedanism (the
common European term for Islam in the late
19th and early 20th centuries), Hinduism,
Buddhism, and Confucianism, among others,
forcing their colonial subjects, through various
bureaucratic means, to identify themselves

primarily in terms of the new categories they created.[10] In this regard, Smith argues that our contemporary notions of religion are radically different from those held by the personalities we identify as the founders of the world's major religions, such as the Buddha, Abraham, Jesus, and Muhammad. In other words, these individuals would not recognize the 'religions' the world associates with them today. Smith consequently devotes much of his book to tracing the complex processes by which fluid conceptions of personal faith, experience, and practice attributed to these founding personalities were gradually abstracted and systemized as religion.

Smith also brings to our attention another aspect of the nature of religion. He argues that since every religion is necessarily located within the context of human history, it is part of the mundane but constantly changing and evolving world of humanity. As a result, it is never fixed; it is unstable, dynamic and evolving, strongly influenced by and influencing the milieu in which it is situated. He points out that we can observe every religious tradition changing over time, with each generation of believers adding to the 'cumulative tradition', representing a broad range of understandings and practices influenced by contexts. This cumulative tradition sets the context and conditions but does not determine the understandings and practices of the next generation. In this sense, all religions are cumulative traditions composed of multiple layers.

Carl Ernst, in his book *Following Muhammad*, similarly emphasizes the idea that we must contextualize representations of religion:

> Religion never exists in a vacuum. It is always interwoven with multiple strands of culture and history that link it to particular locations. The rhetoric of religion must be put into a context, so that we know both the objectives and the opponents of particular spokespeople.[11]

He further points out that by adopting an approach that pays close attention to the multiple and ever-changing contexts within which a religion is located, it is impossible to conceive of a religion, at least in an academic context, to be a fixed object, a conception which scholars of religion call 'reification' or 'objectification'. When notions of religion become reified, people personify them or give them agency by declaring, for instance, 'Islam says . . .', or 'according to Islam . . .'. As Ernst correctly observes, 'No one, however, has ever seen Christianity or Islam do anything. They are abstractions, not actors comparable to human beings.'[12]

A fundamental premise of the cultural studies approach is that the lack of religious literacy fuels antagonism and prejudice against particular groups. While this is certainly true of different religious communities misunderstanding and mischaracterizing each other, it is also equally true within a religious tradition in which differing beliefs, practices, and interpretations among adherents can often lead to suspicion and antagonism, with one party arguing that the other has failed to recognize the true tenets of the faith. By emphasizing that every religious tradition is composed of multiple communities of interpretation, the cultural studies approach gives us a vocabulary with which to frame this problem. It helps us to think about issues of representation by allowing us to recognize how interpretations associated with powerful and dominant groups can come to be considered as 'orthodox' or 'mainstream' while those of less powerful or marginalized groups are sidelined and perceived as heretical. Through the cultural studies approach, for example, we will see that the widespread and popular notion of the five pillars of Islam emerged initially within a Sunni theological context and we will understand that its current hegemony as an 'orthodox' or correct doctrine of Islam can partially be explained by the triumph of Sunni-oriented dynasties in the 12th century over the Fatimids, a Shiʻi dynasty that promoted a 'seven-pillar' analogue. If the Fatimids – whose empire in its heyday encompassed substantial portions of the Middle East, including the holy cities of Mecca, Medina, Qayrawan, and Jerusalem – had managed to triumph over their rivals, we might today have a very different definition of orthodoxy. Power is consequential; it is the victorious who shape how history is narrated.

If we change our analytical lens from the theological to the sociopolitical, we can consider the interplay between historical contexts and ideologies of power, such as colonialism and nationalism, in shaping contemporary expressions of Islam. For instance, a Muslim woman living in Taliban-controlled regions of Afghanistan, where pre-Islamic, highly patriarchal Pashtun tribal codes mandate that women cover themselves from head to toe, experiences her religion very differently from a Muslim woman who chooses to wear a headscarf in Turkey, where it is perceived by secularists as a symbol of religious fundamentalism. In Senegal, Sufi orders espousing a mystical interpretation of Islam exercise significant political and economic influence, whereas in Saudi Arabia, such organizations are banned as heretical and contrary to the state's official religious ideology. Similarly, the experience of being a Uighur Muslim in China – a state that is officially atheistic and considers its Uighur populations to be ethnic minorities who have to be assimilated to mainstream Han culture – differs from that of being a Muslim in Pakistan, a Muslim-majority state in which the invocation of Islam as the underlying ideology for the state has led to violent sectarian conflict. In Western contexts, we can look at the experiences of Muslims of Turkish origin in Germany or North Africans in France who have been marginalized in their adopted countries on account of their race and religion and contrast them with those of African Americans in the United States, some of whom, such as Malcolm X, have regarded Islam as an alternative to Christianity in asserting their distinctive identity in their struggle against racism and for civil rights. The political and social contexts in which a Muslim practises his or her faith are just as important or, some would argue, even more important than doctrines and rituals in determining how

Figure 4. Malcolm X
Malcolm X is shown, here, holding a newspaper with the headline 'Our Freedom Can't Wait'. The photo was taken at a rally in New York, 1963.

contemporary Muslims experience and interpret their faith.

Key to the cultural studies approach is an appreciation of the full range of discourses through which Muslims have expressed their beliefs, particularly those that may have been marginalized. Thus, we cannot restrict ourselves only to representations of Islam that have gained prominence because they dominate media, social, political, and academic spaces. In this regard, Mohammed Arkoun characterizes representations of Islam amplified in these spaces as 'loud Islam', one that is elitist and predominantly portrays the religion as an ideology of revivalism, identity formation, and political legitimation.[13] He further asserts that these are, in reality, secular movements 'disguised by religious discourse, rites, and collected behaviors'.[14] As a result of their domination, hardly any attention is given to understanding the way in which the faith of Islam is practised and, indeed, experienced by the majority of the world's Muslims. Simply put, the living Islam of the faithful and how they understand, express, and experience their individual relationship with the transcendent have been ignored or marginalized. Hence, Arkoun refers to this as 'silent Islam'.[15] As the majority of the world's Muslims experience their faith through various arts, they can provide powerful lenses through which we can appreciate experiences of Islam that have been marginalized or silenced. Thus, Quran recitations, calligraphy, poems, folk songs, dance, short stories, novels, miniature

Figure 5. Mohammed Arkoun
Portrait of Mohammed Arkoun. Arkoun wrote about 'loud Islam' and 'silent Islam' as ways in which Muslims express their religion.

paintings, films, and architecture can all offer valuable insights into Muslim faith perspectives.

Centring the Diversity of Islam

A cultural studies approach to the study of Islam recognizes that the experiences and expressions of any religion are far from homogeneous or monolithic. Every religious tradition is marked by internal diversity, tensions, and contradictions, manifested through diverse communities of interpretation. In the course of historical evolution, a dazzling variety of interpretations, rituals, practices, and artistic expressions have come to be associated with the faith of Islam. Indeed, many Muslims whose understanding of their religion is restricted to their specific devotional and sectarian contexts are astonished when they become aware of this diversity. Some are even threatened by it and vehemently claim that there is only one true Islam – the one they believe in. Others emphasize that all Muslims are united by certain fundamental common beliefs such as those expressed through the *shahada* (the Islamic profession of faith), in which a Muslim declares that there is only one God, and that Muhammad is His Prophet. However strong the desire to reduce or simplify Islam to a few common beliefs or rituals, the historical reality is that the religion, and even its fundamental creed, has come to be interpreted in diverse ways depending on each region's history and cultural traditions, its economic and political structures, and its geography. We cannot dismiss the crucial and incontrovertible historical evidence that, as the Islamic tradition evolved after the Prophet Muhammad's death and spread to many different regions and cultures, ranging from Albania and China to Yemen and Zanzibar, it came to have different significations for different groups, both Muslim and non-Muslim alike. We may even think of Islam as an umbrella term overarching layers of meaning or even as a rainbow-like spectrum consisting of many distinctive colours.

The diverse ways in which we can explore Muslim interpretations and expressions of their faith highlight for us the importance of recognizing that the story of Islam is not one story, but many stories involving peoples of many different races, ethnicities, and cultures. This perspective helps us interweave the voices of poets, novelists, short-story writers, folk musicians, and rock stars with those of clerics, theologians, mystics, scholars, and politicians in order to create a nuanced picture of the rich and multicoloured tapestry we call Islam. Each of these stories is also set in specific contexts and bound by the immediate circumstances of its location in historical time and space.[16] Therefore, asking what a religion teaches is no longer a viable question in itself as it will solicit a range of answers. In order to distinguish between competing interpretations and claims, the crucial questions one should ask include: 'Which Islam?' 'Whose Islam?' 'Who is interpreting it?' 'On what basis of authority?' and 'In which context?' Such questions will explicitly and implicitly frame the discussions in this book as we explore the shared commonalities as well as the fissures and disagreements between Muslim communities on issues that have become central to constructing understandings of their faith.

Chapter 1

Who is a Muslim?

Several years ago, one of my students, Elizabeth, an ordained Christian minister, was engaged in conversation with Fatima, a Muslim woman, regarding the basic doctrines of Islam. In the midst of their discussion, Fatima proclaimed, 'You too are a Muslim.' Elizabeth was surprised, even a little shocked. 'How so?' she inquired, 'You know I am a Christian.' Fatima responded, 'I consider anyone who commits themselves to God to be a Muslim; this is what the word literally means.' That the two women understood the term 'Muslim' in different ways may at first glance seem surprising, even awkward. However, over the centuries, Muslims themselves have understood the terms 'Islam' and 'Muslim' differently, their understandings being shaped by their individual contexts and 'situatedness', be they theological, legal, historical, or political. This chapter will use the cultural studies approach to not only explore some of the multiple ways in which the terms 'Islam' and 'Muslim' have been interpreted, but also how they have been dynamically fashioned and refashioned over time and across geographical locations. In the following section, we will look

at four different and established responses to the
question 'Who is a Muslim?'

A Muslim is a Person Who Follows
the Religion of Islam

Today when we conventionally use the word
'Muslim', we employ it to identify a person who
is a follower of Islam or a believer in Islam.
Religion, in this case Islam, is conceived of as a
system of beliefs and practices commonly shared
by a community of individuals. On this premise,
we often categorize the world's population into
distinctive faith-based communities according
to the religions they espouse. Viewed from this
perspective, the word 'Muslim' also serves as a
marker of communal identity.

Almost all Muslims assert that the *shahada*
represents the doctrinal boundaries of the *umma*
(community of Islam). Usually recited in Arabic,
the *shahada* comprises two phrases: 'There is
no god but God' and 'Muhammad is the messenger of God'. According to most schools of Islamic
theology, anyone who genuinely affirms the
beliefs expressed in the *shahada* is a Muslim.
The *shahada* has both inclusive and exclusive
aspects. The first phrase, 'There is no god but
God', is inclusive in character in the sense that
anyone who is a monotheist may ascribe to
it. The second, 'and Muhammad is the messenger of God', is exclusive, for it sets apart
monotheists who believe in the prophethood
of Muhammad from those who do not. As a
result, belief in Muhammad's message and the

Figure 6a. The Shahada al-Tawhid (Unification Fountain)
The sculpture of granite and marble, located in Jeddah, Saudi Arabia, is an
architectural depiction of the *shahada*, the Islamic profession of faith.

Figure 6b. Shahada Calligraphy at the Blue Mosque, Istanbul, Turkey
Plaque with the *shahada* mounted on the wall of the mosque.

affirmation that he is the last of God's prophets, 'the seal of prophets', have become the distinctive hallmarks of Islamic identity.

Although the definition of a Muslim as a person who professes Islam as a religion is universal today, when the Prophet Muhammad first began preaching his message in seventh-century Arabia, he and his followers did not understand the words *muslim* and *islam* in this manner. Undoubtedly, this statement may seem surprising to many readers, especially to Muslims who consider 'Islam' to be the special name that God gave to their religion. However, as we shall discuss in detail, the Quran does not associate the terms *muslim* and *islam* with a specific religion. Rather it uses the term *muslim* to mean 'one who has submitted [to the one God]' and *islam* to mean 'submission [to the one God]'. In this sense, it regards Abraham, Moses, and Jesus as *muslim*s and considers their followers to be *mu'minun* (believers). Moreover, while the Quran affirms the core teachings expressed in the *shahada*, it does not specifically mention the *shahada* as a credal formula of a specific religion called 'Islam'. This formulation seems to have developed several years after Muhammad's death as the need arose among some of his followers to differentiate themselves socially and politically from Jews and Christians who also ranked among the believers (*mu'minun*). According to the historian Fred Donner, the emergence of the term 'Islam' as the name of a specific religion can be traced to the early eighth century, when members of the

Umayyad dynasty reinterpreted key terms from the Quran to legitimize their imperial power by linking that power to divine revelation and their role as successors (*khalifas*) to the Prophet Muhammad. In the process, they came to interpret Islam as a triumphalist religiopolitical ideology that focused on the Prophet and the Quran, and that superseded the traditions that preceded it.[1]

To throw further light on the later historical evolution of the term 'Islam' as the name of an organized religion, Wilfred Cantwell Smith examined the titles of some 25,000 Arabic works written by Muslims over 12 centuries. His research revealed that it was only since the latter part of the 19th century that Muslims predominantly came to think about their religion in an institutionalized sense. Since that time, the notion of Islam as a religious and sociopolitical ideology has gained popularity, and concepts such as *iman* (faith in God) and *mu'min* (believer) – which were prominently employed by earlier generations of Muslims – have dramatically declined in usage. In other words, as Muslims increasingly conceived of 'Islam' in ideological terms, the focus on God and faith receded. In explaining this gradual shift, Smith suggests that the conception of Islam as an ideal religious system, and later as a civilization, is the result of Muslims attempting to defend and articulate their faith and beliefs within European colonial contexts, incorporating Western conceptions of religion and the idea of secularism. He writes:

> On scrutiny it appears that the almost univer-
> sal Muslim use of the term *islam* in a reified
> sense in modern times is a direct consequence
> of apologetics . . . the impulse to defend what
> is attacked would seem a powerful force
> towards reifying. This process has clearly
> been at work in the Islamic case.[2]

In support of Smith's assertions, Ernst observes
that Orientalists, such as E. W. Lane, first introduced the use of the term 'Islam' as the name of a
religion into European languages in the early 19th
century as an alternative to the 'Mohammedan
religion' or 'Mohammedanism', both European
terms which Muslims today find offensive. As
employed by Europeans, 'Islam' was meant to be
analogous to the modern Christian conception of
religion. Ernst further asserts:

> The use of the term 'Islam' by non-Muslim
> scholars coincides with its increasing
> frequency in the religious discourse of those
> who are now called Muslims. That is, the term
> 'Islam' became more prominent in [Muslim]
> reformist and protofundamentalist circles at
> approximately the same time, or shortly after,
> it was popularized by European Orientalists.
> So in a sense, the concept of Islam in oppos-
> ition to the West is just as much a product
> of European colonialism as it is a Muslim
> response to that European expansionism.[3]

The conception of 'Islam' as an exclusive religious ideology provided, in certain circumstances,

the basis for the development of a theology that promoted the idea of Islam as a religion of empire to legitimize the claims of several dynasties to political hegemony in various regions of the Middle East, South Asia, and sub-Saharan Africa. It also led to the conception that 'Islam' was a fully developed ideology that had been revealed to the Prophet Muhammad as a perfect system of beliefs and practices, and that it was thus outside the process of normal historical development. Such a view perpetuates what the historian Ahmet Karamustafa termed 'the cocoon theory of Islamic civilization', since it refuses to accept the significant ways in which the variegated cultures of the Near East, Asia, and Africa have been incorporated into many aspects of Muslim life and thought, including its theology:

> Islam, it is often observed, came into this world fully grown, and, to boot, in full daylight: a holy book, a prophet, a divine law – all introduced into this world from another world, like a potent drug injected into the body. Exceptionally, however, this drug – which is 'true Islam' – does not interact with the body and is only efficacious when it is preserved intact in its pure and pristine state.[4]

From a historical perspective, the premise of an unchanging and monolithic Islam ignores the reality that Muslims have interpreted their religion in many different ways. There have always been significant doctrinal differences amongst

Muslims even with regard to beliefs that we would consider as core or fundamental to Islam, such as the *shahada*. Often invoked as an ideal symbol of Islamic unity, the *shahada* has been understood differently by various groups of Muslims depending on their specific theological and cultural contexts. The Shi'a, for example, include in their *shahada* a third phrase: 'Ali is the friend of God', to reflect their belief in the nature of authority and leadership of the Muslim community. According to them, after the death of the Prophet Muhammad, religious and temporal authority was the prerogative of Ali, the husband of the Prophet's daughter Fatima, and, following him, that of his direct descendants – the Imams. These Imams alone had the spiritual knowledge and insight to guide believers on matters of faith. Hence, from a Shi'i perspective, affirmation of Ali's authority and that of the Imams is crucial to the correct understanding of the faith and merits inclusion in the *shahada*. On the other hand, mystically inclined Muslims have understood the *shahada* in an esoteric sense, interpreting the phrase 'There is no god but God' to mean that only after negation of the vain and selfish human ego ('There is no god') can one affirm that there is but one real ego – God – to whom all should submit. For them, the phrase encapsulates the true meaning of *islam*: submission of the human ego to God. In other contexts and circumstances, Muslims have attached to the *shahada* a variety of political significations. Historically, many Muslim rulers had the *shahada* inscribed on their coins as a way of legitimizing their right to rule. In more recent times, Afghanistan and Saudi Arabia have employed the *shahada* on their flags to promote Islamic identity, nationalism, and solidarity among its citizens.

A Muslim is One who Submits to the Will of God

In contrast to those Muslims who hold that the word 'Muslim' denotes a follower of Islam, there are others, like Fatima who was mentioned above, who believe that its primary significance lies in denoting a personal relationship between each created being and God. At the heart of this relationship, as we have seen above, lies a conception of *islam* not as a systemized religion but as a private act of faith – the act of submission or commitment to God – symbolized physically by the prostrations which Muslims perform during their ritual prayers. This interpretation is based on the meanings of the words *islam* and *muslim* as they commonly appear in the Quran. Linguistically, both words are derivatives of the Arabic verb *aslama* (to submit, to surrender); *islam* is a verbal noun that signifies the act of submission, while *muslim* is the noun of agency, referring to one who submits.[5] While the term *islam* can be used in Arabic to refer to submission in a variety of senses, such as the surrender of a city or an army, in a theological context it signifies submission to God, and a *muslim* is one who has submitted to God. Historically speaking, this was the sense in which these terms were first used and understood by the Prophet Muhammad and his early followers.

A survey of Quranic verses in which these terms occur indicates that it is not only perfectly acceptable to read *islam* as signifying submission and *muslim* as signifying submitter, but that, in the majority of instances, these are clearly the only meanings intended. For instance, the prophet Abraham (Ibrahim in Arabic), the great patriarch of the three monotheistic faiths – Judaism, Christianity, and Islam – is declared to be a *muslim* in the Quran: 'Abraham was not a Jew or Christian but an upright man who had submitted [*musliman*]' (Q. 3:67). This is, likewise, the case in *Surat al-Baqara*, the Quran's second chapter:

> When his [Abraham's] Lord said to him, 'Submit' [*aslim*], he said, 'I have submitted [*aslamtu*] to the Lord of the Worlds.' And he [Abraham] enjoined his sons as did Jacob: 'O my sons, God has chosen the religion for you; do not die except as *muslims*/submitters [*muslimuna*].'
>
> (Q. 2:131–132)

Seen from this perspective, the story common to the Jewish, Christian, and Islamic traditions recounting Abraham's willingness to sacrifice one of his two sons in response to a divine command represents, in fact, a test of the sincerity of his submission (*islam*) to God. In the Quran, submission to the Almighty is an act not limited to humans, but extended to everything in creation:

Have you not seen how to God bow down
all who are in the heavens and the earth, the
sun and the moon, the stars and the moun-
tains, the trees and the beasts, and the many
of humankind?

(Q. 22:18)

In the context of this interpretation, the primordial path of submission to God, which the entire
universe follows, was preached by a long line of
prophets before Muhammad. Although these
prophets have, over time, come to be associated
with communities that appear to follow different paths or religions, the prophets are
represented in Quranic discourse as having
preached identical messages. Hence, the Quran
commands Muhammad and his followers:

Say: 'We believe in God and in what has been
sent down to us and to Abraham, Ishmael,
Isaac, Jacob and the tribes. We believe in what
was given to Moses, Jesus, and the prophets
from their Lord. We do not make a distinction
between any of them. It is to Him that we are
*muslim*s/submitters [*muslimuna*].'

(Q. 3:84)

Based on this broad understanding of the term
islam, anyone who submits to God is a *muslim*.
According to the Quran, God sent a prophet to
every people and every nation. Popular tradition claims that God has sent as many as 124,000
prophets. Since submission to God was a central

precept in each prophet's teaching, a Jew, a Christian, or a follower of any religion who submits to the one God could be called a *muslim*. It is awareness of this inclusive connotation of the terms *islam* and *muslim* that led the German poet-philosopher Johann Wolfgang von Goethe to declare, in words that sound as provocative today as when he first wrote them: 'If *islam* means submission to God, we all live and die in *islam*.'[6]

While the understanding of *islam* as symbolic of the essential relationship between all creatures and God permeates the Quran, there are a few verses in which the meaning of the term is ambiguous:

> If someone desires other than *islam* as a religion/path (*din*), it will not be accepted of him.
>
> (Q. 3:85)

> Today I [God] have perfected your religion/path (*din*) for you, and I have completed My blessing upon you, and I have approved *islam* for your religion/path (*din*).
>
> (Q. 5:3)

Is the term *islam* in these verses referring to the broader meaning of submission, or to the more specific sense of the name of a religion? Recognizing the complexities of translating this term into English, Muhammad Asad makes the following remark in the introduction to his translation of the Quran:

Throughout this work I have translated the terms 'muslim' and 'islam' in accordance with the original connotation, namely, 'one who surrenders [or has surrendered] himself to God,' and 'man's self-surrender to God' . . . It should be borne in mind that the 'institutionalized' use of the terms – that is, the exclusive application to the followers of Prophet Muhammad – represents a *definitely post-Qur'anic development and hence must be avoided in a translation of the Qur'an* [my emphasis].[7]

Not all Quran translators have displayed such a nuanced contextual interpretation of the terms *muslim* and *islam*. Frequently, under the influence of their particular political and theological outlook, personal interpretative biases inevitably creep into their translations. Let us examine, for instance, the verse 'Verily religion/path (*din*) in the eyes of God is *islam*' (Q. 3:19). Early generations of Quran commentators, including al-Tabari (d. 923), who is among the most respected and authoritative, interpreted *islam* as obedience or submission to God, that is, as an act of faith. In contrast, later commentators and many contemporary Muslims have interpreted the verse in an exclusivist sense, taking it to refer to the religion of Islam as revealed to the Prophet Muhammad.[8] The meaning of the verse is further complicated in that the Arabic word *din*, generally rendered into English as 'religion', has a much wider range of meanings than the translation allows. Smith, in his aforementioned study *The Meaning and End of Religion*, identifies various senses in which early Muslim communities understood *din*, including notions such as 'customs' and 'way of life'. The interpretation of *din* as 'religion', he points out, was only a much later development. And yet, he argues, even this aspect of *din* as 'religion' lacked the exclusivist overtones that we associate with the term today.[9] In its Quranic context, therefore, *din* does not imply 'religion' in the ideological sense, but rather evokes some of the other meanings that Smith notes.

A Muslim is One who is Grateful to God

During a discussion I had with a group of Muslim students on the portrayal of God in the Quran, a student from Texas, Zahra, commented that the God of the Quran was 'hurt' or pained by human ingratitude. A pervasive theme in the Quran, she explained, was a forgetful humanity constantly rejecting the many favours and blessings of the Creator. She cited various Quranic verses in support of her viewpoint:

> We [God] established you on the earth and provided you with the means of livelihood – small thanks you give!
>
> (Q. 7:10)

> Your Lord is bountiful to people, though most of them are ungrateful.
>
> (Q. 27:73)

There was a sign for the people of Sheba
. . . : 'Eat from what your Lord had provided
for you and give Him thanks, for your land
is good, and your Lord most forgiving.' But
they paid no heed. . . . In this way We [God]
punished them for their ingratitude – would
We punish anyone but the ungrateful?

(Q. 34:15–17)

Elaborating further, Zahra remarked that, for her,
the verses which most poignantly depicted God's
lament over human ingratitude occurred in *Surat
al-Rahman* (Q. 55). There, several verses have the
refrain 'Which of the favours of Your Lord will
you deny?' Based on these verses, she opined that
the most important characteristic of a *muslim* is
always remembering to be grateful to God.

This perspective is not unique to Zahra. It
represents a strand of interpretation that is
centuries old. It is manifest in the way in which
many Muslims will respond to greetings such as
'How are you?' by saying *al-shukr li'llah* (thanks
be to God) or *al-hamdulillah* (praise belongs to
God), even if they may be unwell or facing a
distressing situation. They do so with the belief
that expressing gratitude to God is a sign of faith,
especially in times of adversity.

To appreciate more fully how gratitude to
God has come to be the defining characteristic of
a person of faith, it is important to examine
briefly the conception of faith (*iman*) in Islamic
theology. Most Muslim theologians draw a
sharp distinction between *iman* and *islam*

(submission), pointing out that the two are not synonymous. In support of their contention, they usually cite the following Quranic verse:

> The Bedouins say, 'We have faith [*iman*].' Say, 'You do not have faith, rather you say, "We have submitted," for faith has not yet entered your hearts. If you obey God and His Messenger, He will not diminish anything of your works.'
>
> (Q. 49:14)

Commentators explain that while the Bedouin nomads mentioned in the verse may have submitted to the authority of the Prophet Muhammad, and through him to the authority of God and His commands, this did not signify that they necessarily had *iman* (faith) in their hearts. Becoming a *muslim* (one who submits) does not automatically mean that one is a *mu'min* (believer) since submission may, in fact, be an act of political and social expediency or the first step of a journey of exploration for the spiritually nascent.

In the Quran, faith (*iman*) and a person of faith – that is, a believer (*mu'min*) – are often contrasted with their antonyms, *kufr* and *kafir*, terms usually translated as 'infidelity' and 'infidel', respectively.[10] Derived from the Arabic verb *kafara*, meaning 'to reject' or 'to be ungrateful', the noun *kafir* means literally 'one who rejects or who is ungrateful'. Thus, *muslim*s submit to God and His prophets, and the faithful (*mu'minun*) approach God with gratitude in their hearts, while *kafir*s arrogantly reject God's commands out of ingratitude. God, according to this interpretation, does not love those who are arrogant and egotistical. Gratitude to God is, therefore, central to the Quranic conception of faith (*iman*); a person who believes is/is expected to be grateful (*shakir*), and the grateful ones are looked upon favourably by God, as indicated in the Quranic verses below:

> God will reward the grateful.
>
> (Q. 3:144)

> Does not God know best who are the grateful ones?
>
> (Q. 6:53)

> You should worship God alone and be one of those who are grateful to Him.
>
> (Q. 39:66)

Various prophets are represented in the Quran as grateful servants of God, inspiring their followers through their acts of submission (*islam*), faith (*iman*), and thanksgiving:

> Abraham was truly an example: devoutly obedient to God and true in faith. He was not an idolater; he was grateful for the blessings of God who chose him and guided him to the right path.
>
> (Q. 16:120–121)

[God said,] Work, O family of David, in gratitude, for few of My servants are truly grateful.

(Q. 34:13)

Complete and overwhelming gratitude to God is
such an important marker of faith and closeness
to Him that the Spanish Muslim mystic Ibn
Abbad al-Rundi (d. 1390) considered it to be the
highest spiritual station a person could reach. A
human being, he said, should first thank God
with the tongue, then with the heart, until the
whole being is transformed in gratitude and
every moment of life consists of gratitude
towards the Lord. He wrote:

Our whole occupation and only practice
should be to consider God's kindness toward
us, and to think that our might and power is
nothing, and to attach ourselves to God in a
feeling of intense need for Him, asking Him
to grant us gratitude.[11]

The most important way of expressing gratitude to
God is through praise. Notable in this regard is the
first chapter of the Quran, *Surat al-Fatiha*, or 'The
Opening', which includes the oft-repeated phrase
by Muslims *al-hamdulillah*, 'praise belongs to
God'. Writing about this phrase, Sachiko Murata
and William Chittick make the following remark:

Notice that this phrase, 'Praise belongs to
God,' is not an exclamation, although people
may employ it as such. It is not the equival-

ent to the English sentence 'Praise be to God!' which would be uttered on a special occasion. Rather it is a simple statement of fact. No one else deserves praise, because no one else is the source of good and benefit. Everything positive and praiseworthy comes from God, even if talent or the weather or luck seem to be the immediate cause.[12]

It is with exactly these sentiments in mind that many Muslim parents teach their children to respond to praise with the phrase *al-hamdulillah*. Whenever they see something in nature that is beautiful, they should say *al-hamdulillah* or even *subhan Allah* (Glory be to God).

Figure 7. Muslims Praying
Male and female pilgrims praying the afternoon prayer (*asr*) together in congregation just outside Masjid al-Haram, Mecca, Saudi Arabia.

The idea that gratitude to God is a mark of faith, while ingratitude is a mark of infidelity, is beautifully captured in the following prayer that appears in a 17th-century manuscript of Shi'i devotional literature:

O Our Lord!
Let thanks for your bounties
Be the litany of our tongues
And shelter us from the nethermost hell
Of ingratitude and thanklessness.[13]

Expressing gratitude to God, according to some Quranic verses, is a universal phenomenon:

The seven heavens and the earth and every-one in them glorify Him. There is not a single thing that does not glorify Him with praise but you do not understand their praise.

(Q. 17:44)

Do you not see that all those who are in the heavens and the earth praise God, as do the birds with wings outstretched? Each knows its [own way] of prayer and glorification: God has full knowledge of what they do.

(Q. 24:41)

We see this perspective prominently represented in the language of Muslim mystical poetry where we hear God being praised from the most unex-pected corners. One of the characteristics of the enlightened mystic is the ability to hear all of

God's creatures – from the trees and flowers to the birds and fish – praising Him, each creature speaking in *lisan al-hal* (the tongue of its whole being). The Persian poet Sana'i (d. 1131), inspired by the notion that every creature gratefully praises God in its own way, composed a panegyric poem called *Tasbih al-tuyur*, or 'The Rosary of the Birds'.[14] In this poem, he interprets the sounds of each bird species, translating them into human language to demonstrate how all birds constantly praise God through their singing. For example, when the stork says *lak lak*, Sana'i says it is, in fact, praising God by saying (in Arabic) *al-mulk lak al-amr lak*, meaning 'The kingdom belongs to You; the command belongs to You.' Following Sana'i, many Persian mystics have interpreted the pigeon's constant cooing, *ku ku*, as its constant longing for the Divine as it proclaims (in Persian) 'Where is He? Where is He?' Similarly, for Muslim mystics in the Indian subcontinent, the cries of the *papiha* bird (the cuckoo), *piu piu*, represented its searching for God by calling out (in several Indian vernaculars) 'The Beloved, the Beloved'.[15] And from the world of Turkish Muslim mystics comes one of the finest stories illustrating the manner in which it is possible to see all of creation as busy praising God through constant recollection. Sunbul Efendi, the sheikh, or spiritual master, of a mystic order in 16th-century Istanbul was looking for a successor:

> So he sent his disciples to gather flowers to adorn the convent. All of them returned with

large bouquets of flowers; but a certain Merkez
Efendi brought only one small, withered plant
with him. When asked why he did not bring
anything worthy of his master he answered: 'I
found all the flowers busy recollecting the Lord
– how could I interrupt their prayers? I looked,
and lo, one flower had just finished its recollection. That one I brought.' Merkez Efendi
was appointed to succeed Sunbul Efendi.[16]

A Muslim is One Who Adheres to the Five Pillars

Among the most common ways that many define
a Muslim today is by the five pillars of Islam.
Indeed, the statement that all Muslims univer-
sally believe in the five pillars is ubiquitous
in contemporary discourses about Islam.[17] As
popularly understood, the pillars, or *arkan al-din*
as they are called in Arabic, comprise the five
obligations incumbent upon all Muslims: recite
the *shahada*, the profession of faith; perform the
salat, the ritual prayer, five times a day; give
zakat, a prescribed portion of one's income for
charity; observe *sawm*, the daylight fast during
the month of Ramadan; and participate at least
once in the *hajj*, the pilgrimage to Mecca during
the last month of the Muslim year. Underpinning
this five-pillar definition is the conceptualization of ideal and standardized religious practice
which, as we will discuss below, evolved in a
specific context. Today, the pillars have become
the most important yardstick used by many

Muslims (and non-Muslims) to judge an individual's commitment to Islam. Anyone who fails to measure up to this yardstick is considered a lapsed Muslim. In this sense, the five pillars have evolved into a kind of criterion of piety.

Since four of the five pillars are associated with ritual practice, some historians of religion have remarked that as a religious tradition Islam emphasizes orthopraxy (correct practice) in contrast to traditions such as Christianity where the stress is on orthodoxy (correct doctrine). The emphasis on orthopraxy rather than orthodoxy explains why various Muslim religious scholars interviewed by the Munir Commission (1953) in Pakistan found it difficult to agree on the definition of a Muslim as they each had differing notions. It also explains why correct observance of ritual practice has become such an important signifier of proper Islamic identity in many contemporary Muslim societies. It has meant that whenever ultra-conservative groups, such as the Taliban, have sought to 'Islamize' communities, they have done so by insisting that individual Muslims demonstrate their 'Muslimness' through proper practice – observance of the five pillars, especially the daily prayer and fasting during Ramadan. In the eyes of such groups, a Muslim who is ignorant of the five pillars or who does not observe them properly is, in essence, an unbeliever. The five pillars have also, thus, become a means to enforce conformity and hegemonic control.

Despite their significant role as a yardstick for defining Muslim identity today, the terms 'five pillars' or 'pillars of religion' are conspicuously absent from the Quran and other early Islamic texts. However, several verses in the Quran mention certain obligations for those who commit themselves to God, including acts of worship (*ibadat*), such as prayer, fasting, and pilgrimage.

Muslim religious scholars traditionally trace the origins of the five pillars to the *hadith* literature, a genre recording the sayings attributed to the Prophet Muhammad as reported by his close companions and contemporaries. As a corpus, the *hadith* embodies the *sunna*, or custom of the Prophet, which many Muslims have come to regard as a source of revelation complementing or even supplementing the Quran. With regard to the five pillars, we find several *hadith*s, the most important being the following narration attributed to Umar b. al-Khattab, a companion of the Prophet Muhammad who was responsible for codifying many practices during his ten years as caliph (634–644):

> One day when we were with God's messenger, a man with very white clothing and very black hair came up to us. No mark of travel was visible on him, and none of us recognized him. Sitting down before the Prophet, leaning his knees against his, and placing his hands on his thighs, he said, 'Tell me, Muhammad, about submission [*islam*].'
>
> He replied, 'Submission means that you should bear witness that there is no god but God and that Muhammad is God's messen-

ger, that you should perform the ritual prayer, pay the alms tax, fast during Ramadan, and make the pilgrimage to the House [the Ka'ba in Mecca] if you are able to go there.'[18]

Towards the end of this *hadith*, Caliph Umar reveals the identity of the mysterious man in white who questioned the Prophet; he was none other than the angel Gabriel. Notwithstanding this prophetic and angelic endorsement of the five pillars as defining a person's submission to God, there are other *hadith* narratives in which the Prophet Muhammad is reported to have enumerated four or even six pillars. These alternative definitions contained several items, including caring for one's parents, giving one-fifth of the booty from war, and *jihad*, which were excluded from what became the standardized five pillars.[19] Also noteworthy are several *hadith*s which define the term *muslim* in formulations that are outside the framework of the pillars, such as a Muslim is one who does not harm or injure another Muslim. The presence of such texts indicates that even the *hadith* literature contains multiple ways of defining a Muslim.

The five-pillar definition does not find explicit sanction in the Qur'anic text and evidence from the *hadith* is varied. Thus, from the cultural studies perspective several questions arise: How and in what context did the five pillars become a dominant definition of Muslim identity? Who were the individuals and groups who promoted this definition, and on what authority? What were the bases on which they decided that there should be five rather than four or six pillars? Why was caring for one's parents, identified as a pillar in some *hadith*s, not included in the five? What privileged the selection of this particular way of defining Muslim identity over other formulations found in the Quran and *hadith*?

For the moment, most of these questions will have to remain unanswered since much research has yet to be undertaken before we can fully understand the historical development and eventual hegemony of the 'Islam as five pillars' definition. Whatever evidence we do have suggests that the evolution of the five-pillar definition involved a gradual historical process called reification during which fluid conceptions of personal faith, practice, and religiopolitical authority gradually became abstracted, generalized, and systemized into several different interpretations of Muslim practice, with rituals playing a key role in defining boundaries.

By the 10th century, the five-pillar definition appears to have been primarily associated with the Sunni interpretation of Islam. Its principal political champions were the Abbasids; from their capital in Baghdad they ruled a vast empire covering large parts of the Middle East and Central Asia. With the support of Sunni scholars and theologians from the emerging religious establishment they patronized, the Abbasids asserted that they were the sole legitimate caliphs, or rulers, of all Islamdom, an authority they claimed was inherited from the Prophet Muhammad and confirmed by divine will.

Abbasid claims to authority were challenged in the 10th century by the Fatimids, a Shi'i dynasty claiming power to rule over Muslims because they were direct descendants of the Prophet Muhammad through his daughter Fatima and son-in-law Ali. They established an empire in North Africa, eventually founding Cairo as their capital city; from there they propagated their interpretation of Islam. In articulating their version of the pillars of Islam, the Fatimids adopted a framework reflecting their particular interpretation of Shi'i theology, which we now refer to as Ismailism. Based on the teachings of the Prophet Muhammad's great-grandson, Imam Muhammad al-Baqir (d. 743), scholars associated with the Fatimid court asserted that there were seven pillars of Islam. The first and most important of these was *walaya* (devotion to the Imams and the family of the Prophet), followed by *tahara* (purity), *salat* (prayer), *zakat* (tithe), *sawm* (fasting), *hajj* (pilgrimage), and *jihad* (struggle).[20] Moreover, Ismaili theologians, noted for their inclination towards esoteric interpretations, discerned multiple layers of meaning underlying these pillars that were not obvious to the non-initiate. For example, *tahara* (purity) meant not just physical purity but faith untainted by the polluting contagions of doubt and pride, *hajj* (pilgrimage to Mecca) could signify the spiritual journey of the soul, while the *zakat* (tithe) could indicate teaching (as the charitable gift of knowledge).

Viewed within the context of the 10th century, the seven-pillar definition articulated by Fatimid theologians in Cairo presented a Shi'i alternative to the five pillars endorsed by rival Sunni scholars in Baghdad. These two competing formulations constituted one dimension of an intense polemic exchange between two powerful dynasties, one Sunni and one Shi'i, that demonstrated the close link between struggles of political legitimacy and religious practice. The hegemony of the five-pillar definition today marks the triumph of a formulation that is clearly Sunni in origin.

The Shi'i and Sunni tension over the proper practice of Islam becomes even more complex when we realize that there have long been internal differences among the Shi'a. In contrast to the Ismailis, Twelver Shi'i religious scholars chose to articulate religious obligations not in terms of the pillars but as ten 'branches of religion': ritual prayers; fasting during Ramadan; pilgrimage to Mecca when health and finances permit; two forms of almsgiving determined by income (*zakat* and *khums*, the latter being unique to the Shi'a); righteous struggle against vice (*jihad*); enjoining others to do good; forbidding others from doing evil; loving the Prophet Muhammad's family and emulating their deeds; and condemning the enemies of the Prophet's family. Just as there are differences among the Shi'a, there are also differences among the Sunni groups regarding the ways in which their five pillars are to be practised.

In the last century, concern with the observance of the pillars among Muslims acquired an entirely new significance and urgency. Many Muslims, confronted by challenges to their identity and their faith through European colonialism, industrialization, globalization, and the spread of popular Western culture and Western values, have turned to the five pillars as an important means of anchoring their religious identity since they perceive the pillars to be authentic, rooted in history, and stable. Notwithstanding this emphasis on correct ritual practice as a measure of faith, there have always been Muslims who felt that the sometimes zealous tendency to equate a person's adherence to rituals with their commitment to Islam could reduce faith to the performance of rituals without an appreciation of their inner significance. Islamic mystical poetry, for example, contains abundant criticism of those who are preoccupied with defining the human-Divine relationship in strictly ritualistic or legalistic terms. By way of example, here are excerpts from a poem by the famous 11th-century Ismaili Persian poet-philosopher Nasir-i Khusraw. Addressed to a pilgrim who has just returned from Mecca after performing the *hajj*, a ritual that for many Muslims is an important, once-in-a-lifetime experience, the poet, who had performed the *hajj* several times, asks the pilgrim if he had thought about the meaning and significance of each of the rites he performed:

'. . . When you were putting on the pilgrim's robe,
what intention did you resolve in your mind?
Did you promise yourself to make unlawful
everything other than the eternal Lord?'

He said: 'No.' I asked him: 'Did you say
Labbayka! [Here I am!] with full knowledge
   and reverence?
Did you answer God because you heard His
   voice
as did Moses, the interlocutor of God?'. . .

He said: 'No.' I asked him: 'When you hurled
   pebbles
at Satan the accursed, did you throw out
of yourself, at once and completely,
all reprehensible habits and actions?'. . .

He said: 'No.' I asked him: 'During the time
of circumambulation when you were trotting
   like
an ostrich, did you think of the circumambulation'
of the angels around the Supreme Throne?'

He said: 'No.' . . .[21]

Finally, at the end of the poem, when it becomes
apparent that the pilgrim has not understood
the true significance of any of the rites he has
performed, the poet advises him that his pilgrimage has been a wasted effort and that he should
perform it again, but this time with real understanding and proper intention.

Redefining Islamic Values in Colonial Contexts

In more recent times, Western concepts of religion and the nation-state have played a significant role in shaping contemporary understandings of Islam and Islamic values. To appreciate the nature of these influences let us look at two prominent Muslim intellectuals, the Egyptian Rifa'a al-Tahtawi (d. 1873) and the Indian Sir Muhammad Iqbal (d. 1938). Both men lived during an era when Muslim societies in Africa and Asia were being radically transformed by European colonialism, one aspect of what the historian Marshall Hodgson has aptly termed 'the great Western transmutation'.[22] For those Muslims whose understanding of Islam was based on the premise that political power and triumph were signs of divine favour and approval, the loss of political power to the Europeans triggered a crisis of faith. Religious scholars and intellectuals across the ideological spectrum, ranging from ultra-conservative to liberal, addressed the crisis by trying to determine where Muslim societies had gone wrong. Al-Tahtawi and Iqbal were two individuals involved in this reform project.

Al-Tahtawi was a prominent Egyptian religious scholar trained at al-Azhar in Cairo, a premier institution for Sunni Muslim thought. In 1826, he had the opportunity to accompany a contingent of Egyptian students to France as their religious advisor and guide. During the five years he spent in France, he studied various subjects such as ethics, philosophy, mathematics, and geometry. He was impressed by many aspects of French society, including the city of Paris and its hard-working, well-disciplined, and well-educated residents. Upon returning to Egypt, al-Tahtawi is said to have remarked: 'In Paris I saw Islam but no Muslims, but in Egypt I saw Muslims but no Islam.' In his view, although Parisians were not Muslims by faith, their values were nevertheless Islamic. In majority-Muslim Egypt, by contrast, the values al-Tahtawi associated with Islam – hard work, education, discipline, and progress – were absent as most Egyptians were mired in what he saw as illiteracy, laziness, indiscipline, and backwardness.[23] Clearly al-Tahtawi's conception of Islamic values was influenced by his sojourn in France and his exposure to its culture and ideals. On his return home, he became one of the pioneers of the Egyptian reform movement and a leading figure in the movement to foster better understanding between Arab and French civilizations. In the late 19th century, a comment similar to that of al-Tahtawi was attributed to the first Muslim modernist, Muhammad Abduh, who went to Europe in 1888.[24]

Sir Muhammad Iqbal, the eminent South Asian Muslim poet-philosopher of the 20th century, was born in Sialkot (in present-day Pakistan) during the British Raj. As a literary figure, Iqbal was renowned for his Urdu and Persian poetry which ranks among the greatest works of modern Islamic literature and for which he received a knighthood from the British monarch. Almost a decade after his death, his vision of an independent state for the Muslims

Figure 8. Rifa'a al-Tahtawi
Al-Tahtawi was a scholar who applied the principles of Western societies to bring about reform among Egyptian Muslims.

of British India would inspire the creation of Pakistan in 1947. After receiving his initial education in British India, Iqbal travelled to England where he studied at Trinity College, Cambridge, and at Lincoln's Inn in London. Later, he went to Munich University, where he received his doctorate. In 1908, he returned to Lahore to practise law while simultaneously composing poetry in which he expressed his reformist ideas. In his writings, he synthesized his traditional training in the Islamic sciences, including mysticism, with the knowledge he had acquired in Europe, particularly the philosophy of Nietzsche, Bergson, and Goethe. Iqbal's synthesis of these two traditions is best reflected in his concept of *khudi* (selfhood), referring to an intellectually and spiritually invigorated Muslim. This notion was informed by Quranic verses regarding humans as God's vicegerents and by Nietzsche's ideas of the *Übermensch* (superman).

Iqbal's vision of the empowered individual is a central theme in many of his poems, including a two-part Urdu poem called 'The Complaint and the Answer', published 1912–1913. Widely read and recited today, the poem was controversial upon its release for its emphasis on the power of individual human agency. On the basis of such ideas in this and other works, Iqbal's critics accused him of inserting Nietzschean ideas into an Islamic context. In the poem's first part, 'Shikwa' (The Complaint), a frustrated and angry Muslim accuses God of being unjust to the world's Muslims by condemning them to a state of political, economic, and cultural domination by 'infidel' Europeans. In the second part, 'Jawab-i shikwa' (The Answer to the Complaint), Iqbal assumes the voice of God and responds to the angry Muslim devotee. In addressing the specific grievance that God had chosen to favour infidel Europeans over Muslims, Iqbal retorts:

That is a complaint unfounded, and by
     commonsense abhorred;
The Creator's law is justice, out of all eternity –

Infidels who live like Muslims surely merit
Faith's reward.[25]

Iqbal's assertion that God has blessed the infidels
(Europeans) with material triumph ('Faith's
reward') because they 'live like Muslims' is based
on his belief that the Quran teaches that human
beings should constantly develop their God-given
abilities and talents to their fullest potential. Only
then could they properly fulfil their role as God's
'co-creators' and vicegerents in a rapidly evolving
world. For Iqbal, the Muslims of his time had
strayed from these virtues; unlike their ancestors,
who were the embodiment of the spirit of change
and progress, modern Muslims had become conditioned to accept the status quo. As a result,
resignation, self-contentment, lack of initiative,
and sheer passivity had become the principal
characteristics of Muslim societies, leading to their
backwardness and powerlessness. By contrast, the
initiative that Europeans demonstrated in devel-
oping their societies, as well as their emphasis on
maximizing human potential, were characteristic-
ally Islamic virtues. Like al-Tahtawi, Iqbal claimed
that although the Europeans were not Muslims by
faith, they had nevertheless realized the true spirit
of Islam. Why, then, should a just and impartial
God not reward them with triumph as he had
earlier generations of enterprising and progressive
Muslims?

Al-Tahtawi and Iqbal were by no means
uncritical admirers of everything Western or
European. They found fault with what they

saw as the excessively materialistic aspects of
Western societies, especially their selfish pursuit
of wealth and their heedlessness towards the
poor. Iqbal, in particular, was critical of the
exploitative nature of capitalism and colonialism. Yet both men, recognizing the resonance
between their notions of Islamic values and the
positive aspects of European society, expressed
their understandings of Islam in broad universal
terms so that even non-Muslims could embody
the spirit of Islam. In so doing, they were evoking
the broad and inclusive meaning of the term
muslim found in the Quran.

We have seen that, over the centuries, the
words *muslim* and *islam* have acquired a variety
of new significances as their meanings have
been constructed and reconstructed within ever-
changing contexts. What these terms signified to
the Prophet Muhammad in seventh-century
Arabia stands in stark contrast to what they
mean in the highly politicized context of contemporary Pakistan, for example. An important
aspect of this shift, characterized by the process
of reification, was the emergence of distinctive
rituals, such as the *salat* and *hajj*, as markers of
communal identity that distinguished the
followers of Muhammad from other monotheists
(Christians and Jews), and, later, the Sunnis
from the Shi'a. That the decrees of rulers played
a significant role in institutionalizing these practices serves to highlight how closely the process
of reification was tied to the promotion of
specific dynastic ideologies and goals.

Returning to the anecdote with which we began the chapter, it was only when Elizabeth had read more about Islam after her encounter with Fatima, that it dawned on her that her peacemaking companion had based her understanding of the term *muslim* on different criteria from those that had shaped her own. Fatima had regarded her as a fellow submitter to a common God, and, notwithstanding her Christian background, had fully embraced her as a spiritual companion. As Elizabeth reflected on her experience, she wondered how, if even she, who held tolerant views of Islam, found her friend's comment jarring, it would be received by those who blatantly associate the entire Islamic tradition with violence and human rights abuses. Elizabeth wrote in her study-journal:

> When we understand with our rational minds what is happening within a religious tradition across time and space, we can also challenge ourselves and others to confront the gut-level prejudices that are often masked by intellectual tolerance.

Chapter 2

Following God's Beloved: Muhammad as the Ideal Muslim[1]

Every day, millions of Muslims, following the injunctions of the Quran, recite the *salawat*, a formula invoking blessings on the Prophet Muhammad whom they affectionately call 'Habib Allah' (God's beloved). Every year, they also commemorate his birthday, the *mawlid*, by distributing sweets, singing joyful songs, and participating in celebratory processions and

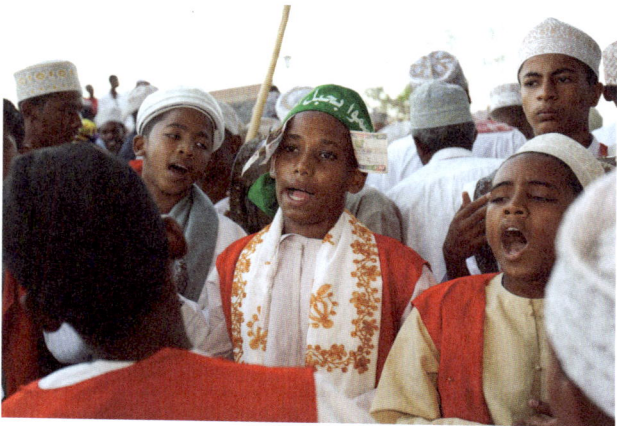

Figure 9a. *Mawlid* Festivities in Song
Swahili boys singing during a *mawlid* in Lamu, Kenya.

Figure 9b. *Mawlid* Festivities in Dance
Mawlid celebration in Paris, France.

Figure 9c. *Mawlid* Festivities, Instrumental Music
Nay (flute) player during a *mawlid* in Luxor, Egypt.

festive events. Through the centuries, Muslims of all theological persuasions and socioeconomic backgrounds have also engaged in the pious act of composing and reciting devotional poems praising the virtues of their Prophet. Written in an astonishing variety of languages, from Azerbaijani to Yoruba, these songs and poems are expressions of the love and esteem that all Muslims feel towards their Prophet. In his Persian poem 'Asrar-i khudi' (The Secrets of the Self), Sir Muhammad Iqbal eloquently describes the relationship between the Prophet and his followers with this verse:

> We are like a rose with a hundred petals
> with one fragrance:
> He is the soul . . . he is the one.[2]

Elsewhere, he declares that love for the Prophet runs like blood through the veins of the Muslim community. Through these evocative images, Iqbal encapsulates one of the key aspects of the Islamic tradition – the central role that the figure of Muhammad plays in unifying a religious community that is otherwise divided by many differences.

Muslims relate to the figure of Muhammad in deeply personal ways. Iqbal aptly described the nature of this relationship when he proclaimed that 'the place of the Prophet is in the heart of a Muslim'.[3] Many Muslims identify so closely with the figure of the Prophet Muhammad that they have internalized him into their very being.

Indeed, as this popular prayer demonstrates, they seek to become like him:

> Unite me with him [Muhammad] as Thou hast united the spirit and soul, outwardly and inwardly, waking and sleeping, make him the spirit of my being under all aspects, in this life as in the next.[4]

Although Islam is a monotheistic faith and Muslims profess submission and commitment to the one God, reverence for Muhammad has become the principal leitmotif of Muslim devotional life and a marker of its distinctiveness. As Constance Padwick aptly points out in her book *Muslim Devotions*, it is simply impossible to truly understand Islam without appreciating the devotion to Muhammad that lies at the heart of many of its traditions.[5] Hence failure to understand the central role that the Prophet Muhammad plays in the lives of his followers has been, and still is, one of the greatest obstacles to an appreciation of Islam. Ironically, the most important factor contributing to the lack of understanding about Muhammad and his relationship to Muslims may lie in the conventional academic approach to this subject. For the most part, studies about Muhammad have been characterized by an overwhelming emphasis on his historical personality. There have been innumerable biographies exploring topics such as his life, influences on his thought, motives for his sociopolitical activism, the development of his consciousness as a

Prophet, and so on. Yet I would argue that to truly understand his significance for Muslims, it would be more fruitful for us to probe the figure of Muhammad as the paradigm, or role model, for Muslim life. The exemplar, the guide, the intercessor, the kind and loyal friend, the beloved, the lover – these are some of the roles that Muslims have seen in their Prophet. In other words, our questions should not centre exclusively upon the historical Muhammad of seventh-century Arabia, the Muhammad of history, but rather upon the Muhammad of faith. By focusing on the Muhammad of faith we are better able to appreciate the various ways in which Muslims living in different historical periods and geographic and cultural contexts relate to their Prophet and the deep devotion he evokes in them. We will see, moreover, that exploring various conceptualizations of Muhammad can be helpful in illustrating the different ways in which Muslims have understood Islam.

In this chapter we will explore some of the different ways in which Muslims relate to the Prophet Muhammad and the several roles he plays in Muslim devotional life. We will consider four themes: his role as prophet and messenger of God; the imitation of his *sunna* (custom) to establish personal, communal, and pietistic norms for Muslims; his role as a much beloved intercessor between his community and God; and speculation about his spiritual status, particularly with regard to the story of his ascension to heaven (the *mi'raj*). Finally, since Muslim understandings of the Prophet are significantly influenced by contexts, we will closely examine two regions, South Asia and China, so that we can highlight the role that different cultural and literary traditions play in shaping conceptions and portrayals of Muhammad.

The Prophet Muhammad and Muslim Devotional Life

Muhammad as God's Prophet and Messenger

Perhaps the best way to begin a discussion about the role of Muhammad in Islamic piety is to start with the second part of the *shahada*, the Islamic profession of faith: 'And Muhammad is the Messenger of God'. At one level, this simple phrase functions as a doctrinal statement that fundamentally differentiates Islam from other monotheistic religions. While all monotheists can affirm the first part of the *shahada* – 'There is no god but God' – only Muslims could subscribe to the second part which entails acknowledgement of Muhammad as one of God's messengers. Hence, belief in Muhammad's prophethood serves as a crucial marker of Islamic identity, distinguishing Muslims as a religious community from other monotheistic communities. At another level, for many, the acknowledgement of Muhammad as God's messenger involves a commitment to obey whatever was revealed to him, including the various religious practices that he established. Thus, from both perspectives, Muhammad is pivotal to defining Islamic identity.

For his followers, Muhammad (born in the Arabian city of Mecca, ca. 570) was sent by God as the 'bringer of good tidings' (Q. 33:45) and as 'a shining lamp' (Q. 33:46) for those who err in the darkness of ignorance, and as a 'mercy for the worlds' (Q. 21:107) to teach God's message to humanity so that it might be guided to the path of righteousness. As a prophet, he represented a tangible figure of authority who could accept allegiance and offerings on God's behalf (Q. 9:103; Q. 58:1) and forgive sins (Q. 5:13; Q. 3:159; Q. 7:199). According to Muslim belief, Muhammad brought to the peoples of seventh-century Arabia the same divine message that had been given to other communities by earlier prophets, all of whom were *muslims* as they had submitted to the one God. As we have already seen, the Quran urges believers to proclaim:

> Say: we believe in God and what has been revealed to us and what was revealed to Abraham, Ishmael, Isaac, Jacob, and the tribes, and in what was given to Moses, Jesus, and the prophets from their Lord. We do not make a distinction between any of them. It is to Him that we are *muslims*/submitters [*muslimun*].'
>
> (Q. 3:84)

Among these prophets, Abraham, Moses, and Jesus are given pride of place. In the Islamic tradition, Jesus is the prophet preceding Muhammad and born of the Virgin Mary, herself considered by some Muslims to have been a prophet through the inbreathing of God's spirit. They do not, however, believe Jesus to be God's son, and according to traditional Muslim belief, he was not crucified, but taken to heaven. According to the Quran, all prophets are members of an extended family whom God has chosen to guide humanity:

> God chose Adam and Noah, the family of Abraham and the family of Imran above all people. Offspring, one from the other, and God hears and knows all things.
>
> (Q. 3:33–34)

Thus, for Muslims, Jesus and Muhammad are both ultimately descended from a shared ancestor, Abraham: Jesus was a descendant of Abraham's son Isaac through his maternal grandfather, Imran, while Muhammad was descended from Abraham's son Ishmael. Besides the 28 prophets mentioned in the Quran, Muslim popular belief acknowledges that before the advent of Muhammad, God had sent many messengers to humanity – as many as 124,000 according to legend – to every nation and to every people. This belief has led some Muslims to include in the category of 'prophet' figures from a variety of religious traditions that preceded the emergence of Islam. Thus, even though they are not specifically mentioned by name in the Quran, some Muslims have considered figures such as Socrates, Plato, Alexander the Great, Krishna, and Confucius to be part of the ancient lineage of prophets who preceded Muhammad. Muslims believe Muhammad to be the last (the 'seal') of God's messengers, to whom was revealed the final instalment of revelation, the Quran (the Recitation) in Arabic. The fact that the Quran was revealed to the Prophet piecemeal over some 22 years (from 610 to 632) underscores the importance of divine guidance being shaped by the need to address changing historical and political contexts.

The Quran, which was codified and organized into 114 chapters several decades after the death of the Prophet, is considered by many Muslims to be God's word. They do not regard Muhammad as its author, but merely as its transmitter. As a Muslim preacher in Kenya explained to his congregation, the Prophet's role was somewhat like a transistor radio. The transistor radio simply picks up the signals and transforms them into sound; it is not the source of the broadcast. Although the transistor metaphor may be simplistic, it illustrates the dominant Muslim viewpoint that prevails today. The Quran, they point out, emphasizes Muhammad's humanity by calling him 'a human being like you to whom revelation was brought' (Q. 41:6).

In contrast to this viewpoint, prevalent historically there have always been Muslim individuals and interpretive communities who, mindful of the complexities of divine revelation, reject the notion that God's message was external to Muhammad and communicated through him in such a mechanical way. To cite a recent example, the late Fazlur Rahman (d. 1988), a leading Pakistani Muslim intellectual, maintained that Muhammad's heart and mind did play a role in shaping the Quran. While accepting the divine origin of the Quran, he maintained that since it is expressed in Muhammad's words, it bears the imprint of his personality. On the basis of Quranic passages that speak of revelation being brought down on the heart of Muhammad, Rahman posits that the Quran was inspired within Muhammad after he had prepared himself for this momentous event by purifying himself from his own faults and reflecting on the errors of his community. In this manner, Muhammad's personality and experiences were so closely intertwined with the nature and process of revelation that the two cannot be separated.[6]

Muhammad as a Beautiful Role Model and Exemplar

Verily in the messenger of God you have a beautiful model for everyone who hopes for God and the Last Judgment and often remembers God.

(Q. 33:21)

In addition to his role as a prophet and messenger, the Quran also describes Muhammad as 'a beautiful model' (uswa hasana). This designation has greatly influenced the manner in which Muslims have come to regard him. He was not simply the bearer of the Quranic revelation but also a divinely endorsed role model who exemplified how to lead a life according to God's will. The implications of this endorsement are profound: as a prophet of God and a bearer of revelation, Muhammad could not have committed an act or said something that contradicted the message he was chosen to reveal. Muhammad was literally a living embodiment of the Quran. According to an oft-repeated saying attributed to Aisha, one of the Prophet's wives and a powerful voice in the early Muslim community, 'Muhammad's nature was the Quran.' She is also believed to have famously declared that he was the 'walking Quran' or the 'Quran on two legs' because he embodied the word of God. As a result of such characterizations of the Prophet, after his death, Muhammad's customary norms (*sunna*) gradually came to form an important basis on which to establish legal, personal, and pietistic norms for the faithful. By the ninth century, when the schools of Islamic law crystallized, Muhammad had come to be regarded as the lawgiver par excellence.

While all Muslims strive towards *imitatio Muhammadi*, they differ amongst themselves regarding those aspects of Muhammad's *sunna* that are obligatory and those that are voluntary. Generally speaking, all that stems from the Prophet concerning the faith, including its prescriptions and practices, is considered obligatory. This is particularly the case with issues about which the Quran is silent or unclear. For instance, as we have seen earlier, the notion of

the five pillars of Islam is based on Prophetic
sunna or custom rather than on explicit Quranic
statements. Similarly, since the Quran stresses
the importance of *salat*, the ritual prayer, without
describing how to perform it, the actions are
determined by Muhammad's reported practice.
Male circumcision is another example of a widespread obligatory practice that is justified on the
basis of Prophetic *sunna*, although it is never
mentioned in the Quran.

The majority of Muslims consider imitating
Muhammad's lifestyle, his likes and dislikes,
his mode of behaviour, and even his habits in
personal hygiene and dress, to be voluntary or
supererogatory. The Prophet's practice of having a
beard has led to significant debate about whether
Muslim men should have one as well. Unlike the
Torah which contains an injunction that some
Jews have interpreted as a command to keep a
beard, the Quran contains no such injunction.
However, on the basis of traditions attributed to
the Prophet, some Muslim men consider growing
a beard to be a religious obligation.

How do Muslims determine the specific details
of the Prophet's *sunna*? From the earliest periods
of his career as a prophet, Muhammad's words
and actions were narrated orally time and again
by his family and by those who were close to
him. After his death, these informal oral reports
were often used to explain and decipher enig-
matic verses in the Quran. As Muslims came to
increasingly emphasize the importance of the
Prophetic custom in determining norms, these

informal accounts became stylized, committed to writing and codified into a distinct literary genre called the *hadith.* As the embodiment of the Prophetic *sunna,* the *hadith* not only confirmed and elaborated on the revelation but also extended it by providing guidance on issues about which the Quran was silent or ambiguous. In this way, the *hadith* functioned not only as a kind of commentary on the Quran but also, sometimes, as an extension of the revelation. Thus, even after his death, through the *hadith,* Muhammad continues to function as the chief and most authoritative interpreter of the Quran.

Muhammad as Beloved Intercessor

O solver of difficulties, listen to my lament,
  listen to my lament.
Despite my trust in you, my world has been
  destroyed.
Have mercy on this destitute one, O Lord of
  Medina.
My destiny adverse, the boat of my life
  trapped in a vortex.
Have mercy on this destitute one, O Lord of
  Medina.
Now is the time to remedy all that has gone
  wrong.
The secrets of my heart are not hidden from
  you.
The heart of this helpless one is full of
  wounds.

Be kind to this destitute one, O Lord of
    Medina.[7]

These lyrics, addressed to the Prophet Muhammad,
are from the famous Urdu song 'Bekas pe karam
kijiye' (Have Mercy on this Destitute One)
composed for the film *Mughal-e-Azam* (1960),
one of the great classics of Bollywood, India's
largest film industry. The film narrates the tragic
love story between the Mughal prince Salim and
a dancing girl, Anarkali. Because their romance
contravened societal norms and conventions,
Salim's father, the Mughal emperor Akbar, deman-
ded an immediate end to their relationship and
ordered Anarkali to be cast into a dark dungeon.
The very poignant soundtrack accompanying
the film was written by the renowned poet and
lyricist Shakeel Badayuni (d. 1970). Its intention
is to portray the despondency of the film's
powerless heroine, and in doing so it provides
us with a glimpse of the role that Muhammad
can play as an intercessor. He is a figure to whom
his devotees can turn at moments of grief and
difficulty.

The Prophet's protection is symbolized by
his cloak or shawl (*burda* in Arabic, *kamli* in
Urdu), which he is said to have thrown around
the shoulders of one of his bitter enemies, Ka'b
b. Zuhayr (d. ca. 630), after the latter repented
for his hostility to the Prophet and composed a
poem imploring his mercy. Hence, the Prophet's
cloak has also come to be viewed as a symbol of
his forgiveness.

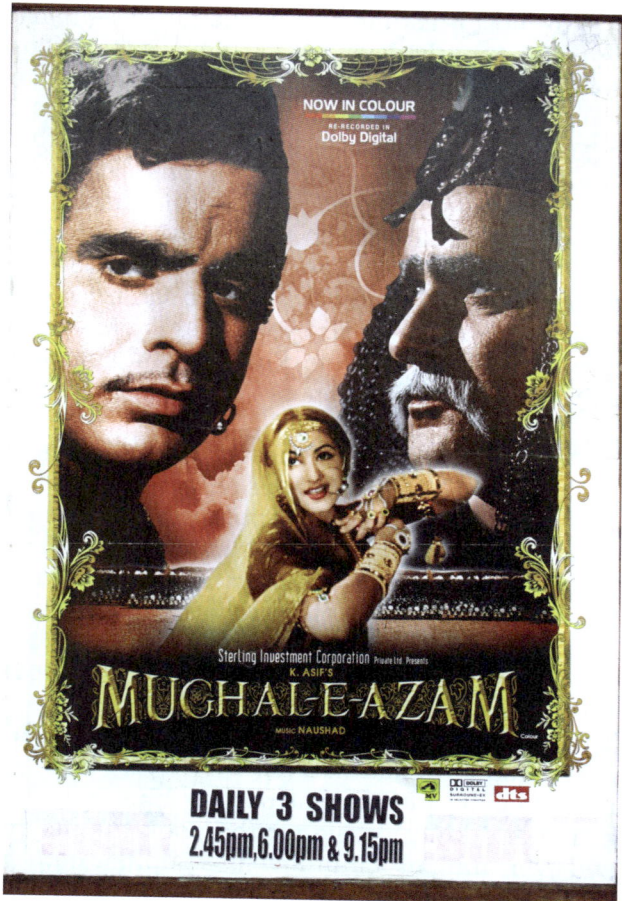

Figure 10. Film Poster for *Mughal-e-Azam*
The soundtrack for this film evokes the Prophet Muhammad's role as intercessor in times of despair.

For most Muslims, it is Muhammad's *shafa'a* (intercession) that symbolizes their belief that as God's beloved and prophet he has the ability to seek God's mercy and forgiveness of their sins. Several factors have led to the emergence of this conviction about the Prophet's intercessory role. First, there are many references in the Quran that indicate that intercession before God is a theological possibility. For instance, the verse of the throne (Q. 2:255) states that no one can intercede with God 'except by His permission'. One verse specifically refers to the Prophet Muhammad's ability to ask for forgiveness:

> We (God) sent no prophet except that he should be obeyed by Allah's permission. And if, when believers had wronged themselves, they would have come to you to seek Allah's forgiveness, and if the Messenger had also asked forgiveness for them, they would have found Allah Forgiving, Merciful.
>
> (Q. 4:64)

The Quranic characterization of Muhammad as a 'Mercy to Nations' (Q. 21:107) as well as numerous narratives that portray him as being gentle and kind, caring for the poor, the needy and even animals, culminate in a popular *hadith* in which God on the Day of Judgment asks him:

> 'O Muhammad, lift your head, ask, and you will be given; intercede, and you will be granted [what you ask].'

I lift my head and say, 'O Lord, *ummati, ummati*, my community, my community!'

And God says: 'O Muhammad, lead into Paradise those from your community who need not undergo reckoning; through the right gate. But in what is beyond that they shall be equal to those that enter through the other gates.'[8]

Generations of Muslims have pinned their hope on this role of Muhammad, who will arrive with a green flag of praise to lead any who have recited the *shahada*, including sinners, to paradise. Indeed, the role of Muhammad as intercessor truly becomes one of the most significant leitmotifs of Prophet-oriented piety. The notion that a penitent sinner can be saved by Muhammad's intercession and God's mercy has led Muslims, ranging from learned scholars and ecstatic mystics to popular minstrels and statesmen, to implore the Prophet's intercession through prayers and verses. Typical of such poems is the following excerpt from 'Ode in Praise of the Messenger', composed by Asma bt. Shehu (d. 1865), the renowned African poetess and scholar also known as Nana Asma'u. In this poem, composed in the West African language Hausa, she pleads for the Prophet's intercession, sometimes referring to him by his alternative name, Ahmad:

O my Lord, cause us to enter into the salvation of the Prophet,

> For the sake of his rank, the best of
>   mankind, Ahmad,
> O our Lord, may we pass over the bridge of
>   Jahannam [hell],
> For the sake of the majesty of our Prophet
>   Muhammad,
>
> . . .
>
> O our Lord, save us on the Last Day from the
>   Fire, take us
> To the dwelling of ease, Paradise, for the
>   sake of Ahmad,
>
> . . .
>
> O our Lord, may we behold Thy presence,
>   the presence of
> The King of the Day of Judgement, for the
>   sake of our Prophet, Muhammad.[9]

Muhammad as Mystic and God's Beloved

The conception of Muhammad as a mystic who enjoyed a privileged relationship with God is primarily associated with accounts concerning the *mi'raj*, or his ascension to the highest heaven and his subsequent meeting with God. Although not described in any detail in the Quran, this event is considered by many Muslims to be the zenith of his spiritual experiences, one that commentators believe is alluded to at the beginning of *Surat al-Isra*:

> Praised be He who travelled by night with
> His servant from the sacred mosque to the

farthest mosque upon which we have sent
down our blessing, that We might show him
some of Our signs.

(Q. 17:1)

The sacred mosque is generally understood to
be Mecca, while the farthest mosque (*al-masjid
al-aqsa*) is commonly interpreted as the Dome of
the Rock in Jerusalem. Another Quranic verse
(Q. 81:22–23) is also said to allude to this event:
'Your companion is not infirm of mind; indeed
he has witnessed him on the clear horizon.'
There are several elaborations of this story in the
biographies of the Prophet in later *hadith* and
legendary material that emerged among his
followers after his death. The gist of the story,
as told by Ibn Ishaq, one of the earliest biograph-
ers, is as follows: One night the Prophet is
awakened by the angel Gabriel and asked to
mount the Buraq, a part human/part animal
winged creature. Riding the Buraq and accompanied by Gabriel, he first goes from Mecca to
Jerusalem (*isra*) where he meets some of the
important prophets who preceded him and
leads them in prayer. He then begins his journey,
described as an ascent, or *mi'raj*, passing through
various heavens, in each of which he meets a
different prophet. Finally, he comes to the
highest heaven where he is blessed with a
beatific vision – a face-to-face meeting with God.

Over the centuries, the account of Muhammad's
journey and visits to the seven heavens, and, in
some cases, to the seven hells as well, has inspired

Muslims to compose a myriad of narratives on this topic. The account has been told both in prose and verse in the many languages Muslims speak, in several cases skilfully incorporating local symbols and motifs so that Islamic concepts are expressed in terms that would be familiar to local audiences. Narratives of the *mi'raj* have also been used to promote and legitimize specific practices and doctrines.[10] Generations of Muslims have pondered the significance of the *mi'raj* and its implications for the human–Divine relationship. Is it to be interpreted as a physical journey or a spiritual allegory? For some, the privilege of meeting/seeing God was unique to Muhammad on account of his special status. Since such an encounter is not possible for ordinary humans, they felt that the best they could do was to emulate and praise the one who was granted this extraordinary experience. For the more mystically inclined, however, this journey, interpreted metaphorically, provides the prototype for the ascent of their own souls to higher spiritual realms. They hold that, like Muhammad, they, too, could have their own *mi'raj* and be blessed with the ultimate reward promised to the faithful in the Quran – being in the presence of God. Based on Q. 53:11–12 ('The heart did not lie in what it saw; will you then dispute with him on his vision?'), they understand the act of seeing not in a physical sense but as 'seeing' or experiencing God in their hearts. According to these mystics, the greatest obstacle to 'seeing' God in the heart is the human ego, since in the presence of God there can be only one ego. Seeing/experiencing God is only possible after the human ego has submitted to God and been cleansed of all negative qualities. It was the submission of the ego to which the Prophet alluded when he said *aslama shaytani*, 'my Satan [ego] has submitted [become *muslim*]'.

Just as a lover totally commits himself to his beloved, so too did Muhammad, out of intense love of God, undergo an internal purification before he could attain the object of his desire. According to Rumi, it was during this process that the fire of divine love burnt away Muhammad's imperfections and enabled him to reach a higher state of illumination and a new life of union with his Beloved. It was only after Muhammad was blessed with the vision of God – the 'utmost limit' in love[11] – that he could experience the presence of the Beloved wherever he turned.

When Muhammad became purified of this fire and smoke of worldly desires, every place he faced was the Face of God.[12]

Here, Rumi refers to the well-known Quranic verse: 'Wherever you turn, you will see the face of God' (Q. 2:115). The experience of seeing God everywhere is only possible when, after the process of self-transformation, one is able to 'see with the heart' the essential existential unity that underlies all of creation. In this sense, the *mi'raj* is, in reality, not an external journey but an internal one into the depths of one's self, culminating in the vision of God. This,

mystically minded Muslims would say, is the
meaning of the Prophet's saying, 'He who knows
himself knows God.'

Another development regarding the nature of
Muhammad's spiritual significance was its association with a form of light mysticism. As early
as the eighth century, the theologian Muqatil b.
Sulayman proposed an esoteric interpretation of
the famous Verse of Light in the Quran:

> God is the Light of the heavens and the earth;
> the likeness of His Light is as a niche wherein
> is a lamp – the lamp in a glass, the glass as
> if it were a glittering star – kindled from a
> Blessed Tree, an olive tree that is neither of
> the East nor of the West, whose oil wellnigh
> would shine, even if no fire touched it: Light
> upon Light; God guides to His Light whom
> He wills. And God strikes similitudes for
> man, and God has knowledge of everything.[13]
>
> (Q. 24:35)

According to Muqatil, the lamp in this verse is a
fitting symbol for Muhammad, who has been
described elsewhere in the Quran as a 'shining
lamp'. Through him the divine light could shine
in the world and guide humanity to the origin
of this light, its true home. On the basis of
this exegesis, other commentators constructed
a theory of light mysticism concerning the
Muhammadan Light, or *nur Muhammad*. In the
celebrated 16th-century Turkish poem 'Mevlid-i
Şerif', which Turkish-speaking Muslims have

regularly recited ever since its composition during celebrations of the Prophet's birthday and on other occasions, the poet Süleyman Çelebi (d. 1411) describes the journey of this Prophetic light. He saw this light as the fountainhead of all prophetic activity, first manifesting itself in Adam, then in all the prophets, one after the other, until it found its full expression in the historical Muhammad.[14]

The notion of a primordial light of prophecy, transmitted serially through all the prophets until reaching its fulfilment in the historical Muhammad, led some of the Prophet's ardent devotees to claim that the cosmic Muhammadan Light was, in fact, the ultimate cause of creation. As proof, they cited a *hadith qudsi* (divine *hadith*) in which God says to the Prophet: 'But for your sake, I would not have created the spheres.' They believed that God created Muhammad from his own light so that Muhammad's spiritual essence, like a column of light, stood before the Lord performing the ritual prayer long before God created everything else from it. This is an idea that is common in Muslim devotional poetry in many different languages and literary traditions. Extolling the brilliance of this light is another popular theme. Asma bt. Shehu, mentioned above, acclaims that the light of Muhammad outshines any other light in its brilliance:

His light exceeds the light of the moon on
    the fourteenth day of the month

Because there is no light like the light of
   Muhammad.[15]

The Prophet Muhammad in Cultural Contexts

People commonly imagine their heroes in terms
of their particular cultural norms and frameworks. As a result, followers of a religious
tradition will understand and represent its principal religious figures in strikingly different
ways, depending on their specific environment.
Among northern Europeans, for example, Jesus
is often portrayed with light-coloured hair and
blue eyes, while in some African churches he is
represented as a black man. Similarly, images
of Mary among different Catholic groups reflect
divergent cultural and artistic aesthetics, ranging

Figure 11a. Northern European Depiction of Mary and Jesus
Stained glass window with Mary and Jesus, Rochester Cathedral, Kent, UK.

Figure 11b. African Depiction of Mary and Jesus
Black Madonna with Jesus, Regina Mundi Church in Soweto, South Africa.

from Our Lady of Guadalupe in Mexico, where she is represented with imagery resonant with the Mexican indigenous tradition, to the Black Madonnas of medieval Europe, which reflect the assimilation of a Christian figure with ancient Greco-Roman earth fertility goddesses.

In her groundbreaking study of the Prophet Muhammad in Muslim devotional life, Annemarie Schimmel observes that the further poets live from Arabia (the Prophet's birthplace), the more eloquent they become in expressing their yearning for him and their desire to visit his tomb in Medina.[16] We can perhaps broaden this remark by observing that in the devotional literatures of Muslims in lands farther from Arabia, we encounter ever more romantic and more exotic images of Muhammad. Many non-Arab Muslims tend to clothe their devotion to the Prophet in metaphors and symbols that reflect their indigenous languages, literary traditions, and cultural norms. Consequently, they surround Muhammad with ideas and themes that may have little or no resonance with doctrines formulated by learned theologians and religious scholars on the basis of Arabian or Near Eastern traditions. In the following section, we will explore the acculturation of the figure of Muhammad to South Asian and Chinese traditions.

South Asian Contexts

As a religious tradition, Islam has flourished so well in the Indian subcontinent that today the region is home to the largest concentration of Muslims in the world. Scholarship on Islam in South Asia has discerned the existence of two distinctive strands: one oriented to Mecca and Arabia and the other oriented to India. The Mecca-oriented strand was often associated with elites who were historically composed of Muslims typically of Arab and Turko-Persian ancestry. Anxious to maintain a distinctive identity tied to their ethnic background and homeland, they looked to Arabia, Persia, and Central Asia for determining the cultural and religious norms of Muslims in South Asia. Since the religion was first revealed in Arabic and developed further in the Persianate tradition, Islamic identity for them was fused with an Arabic or Persian identity. As a consequence, they rejected everything Indian as un-Islamic. Not surprisingly, Muslims espousing this viewpoint extolled the Arabian background of Islam by evoking the example of Muhammad as the Arabian prophet. They highlighted his Arab heritage – that he was Muhammad the Meccan, the Medinan, who belonged to an Arab clan, the Banu Hashim, and the prestigious tribe of the Quraysh.

Intensely at odds with this strand was a more India-oriented one. Representatives of this strand conceived of Islam as a universal religion whose core spiritual concepts could be expressed in any cultural framework. Consequently, not only were they more open to, and tolerant of, the Indian cultural milieu, but they also actively fostered interpretations of Islam that could be more readily understood within the frameworks of local traditions and cultures. Not surprisingly, it was among these esoterically inclined individuals and groups that we witnessed the emergence of a rich tradition in which key Islamic concepts and ideas were 'translated' into regional traditions of folk legends, myths, stories, songs, and poetry.[17]

We can illustrate the process of translation when we consider the different ways in which the figure of the Prophet Muhammad was represented in South Asia's many local traditions. For example, the *punthi* tradition of medieval Bengal sought to introduce the Prophet Muhammad and various Islamic personalities within a framework that drew upon Bengali folk narratives (*mangal kavya*) glorifying and vindicating local deities. A leading figure in this tradition was Saiyid Sultan (fl. 1615–1646), a Sufi *pir*, who composed the *Nabivamsa*, a narrative in which the stories of mythological figures from Bengali epic and hagiographical traditions were presented in a continuum which included prophets and heroes from Adam to Muhammad.[18] This was accomplished by creating an equivalence between the Indic notion of *avatara* (incarnation) and the Islamic concept of *nabi* (prophet). As a result, the Prophet Muhammad came to be understood in this genre as the current and last *avatara* of Vishnu, while Krishna and other *avatara*s of Vishnu were represented as prophets preceding Muhammad.

Among the several indigenous literary motifs used in the *na't* (poetry praising the Prophet), one stands out in particular: the *virahini*, a loving and yearning young woman, usually a young bride or bride-to-be, tormented by the absence of her betrothed. This symbol and the associated concept of *viraha* (longing in separation) enjoyed great popularity in a variety of religious contexts in South Asia where the *virahini* was often identified as a symbol of the human soul. The most renowned use of the *virahini* symbol in Indian devotional poetry occurs in poetry dedicated to the Hindu god Krishna. In this poetry, the *gopi*s (milkmaids), and in particular Radha, express their longings for union with their elusive beloved Krishna.

Within an Islamic context, the *virahini* appears in many literary genres, including the *maulud* tradition in the region of Sindh, today in southern Pakistan. The word *maulud* means 'newborn child', and since the birth of Muhammad was a significant event in the history of humanity, songs composed in his honour came to be called *maulud*. To express their love and affection for the Prophet, Sindhi poets often used the image of the *virahini*. In keeping with literary conventions, a Sindhi poet would represent himself as a *virahini* who can no longer bear the agonies of being separated from her beloved, in this case, Muhammad. Typical of this usage is the following verse by Abd ur-Rauf Bhatti (d. 1752), from 'Maulud 49':

> I am love-sick, beloved, may you be my
> health!
> If the beloved [Muhammad] comes to my
> house, then all pains and afflictions will
> be cured.
> If he curtails the pain, the soul will be at
> peace;

My master, come to me, come to me! An end
   to this separation!
O sweetheart, if I were to meet you, all my
   afflictions would disappear so quickly
O Meccan sir, as dowry, cover the vessel of
   pain
Kissing you on the forehead, I say, may I be
   entrusted to you.
The 'sinful one' Abd ur-Rauf says, 'Grant me
   a place in paradise.'[19]

While this imagery may appear strange by standards of classical Muslim literary traditions in Arabic or Persian – in which it would be rare to conceive of Muhammad as a bridegroom – from the point of view of Sindhi culture such imagery is perfectly conventional. Historically speaking, it was the process of indigenization that was instrumental to the successful dissemination of fundamental Islamic concepts in many parts of South Asia. It allowed Muslims to relate to their Prophet in forms that aroused immediate associations and emotions with their cultural background.

Chinese Contexts

According to a legend popular among Chinese Muslims, a few years before his death the Prophet Muhammad appeared in a dream to Emperor Taizong (d. 649). Muhammad told the emperor that Muslims could be a powerful ally, and that China should expect his representatives. Taizong's successor received the promised delegates in his capital, present-day Xi'an, in 651. Sent by the third Caliph Uthman, the envoys told the new emperor about Allah and presented him with a Quran.[20] According to Muslim sources, he responded positively to their efforts and noted similarities between the message of Muhammad and the teachings of the revered sage Confucius. Though he had no interest in converting, the emperor encouraged the ambassadors to stay in China and tell others about their faith. Though the stuff of legend as much as history, this meeting underscores perceived similarities between the Confucian and Islamic traditions that both the Chinese and the early Muslims must have noted to some extent.

These first Muslims were soon followed by Muslim traders from the Near East, arriving either via the Silk Road or through ocean trade routes that connected the Arabian peninsula with Chinese ports like Guangzhou. By the end of the seventh century, Islam had gained an irreversible foothold in China, long before it took hold in Southeast Asia and, arguably, before it gained a lasting presence in South Asia. The descendants of these traders, known as the Hui,[21] today form the largest group of Chinese Muslims.

From their arrival through to present times, the history of the Hui has been tightly interwoven into the history of Han China. Many Hui Muslims did not view their Muslim identity as something oppositional to, or even independent of, their Confucian surroundings.[22] Rather, they sought to carve out a social and intellectual space that was as much Chinese as it was Muslim.[23] Loyal to the Confucian tradition, it was only appropriate that Chinese Muslims showed reverence for their upbringing and their heritage and followed the way of their forebears.[24] Not surprisingly, Hui Muslims found in the Confucian worldview ample space for Muhammad.

A prophet in Arabia, Muhammad became a sage in China. The parallel was in many ways a natural one; as a wise ruler and a knowledgeable teacher, he fit nicely into a cultural role that had long been revered in Chinese society. Much as Muhammad had stood beside Rama, Krishna, and the Buddha as an avatar of Vishnu in Bengal, he now held ranks with the likes of Shun, Huang Di, and Confucius as a sage of the Dao.[25] Probably best translated as 'the way', the Dao neatly paralleled the notion of the *sirat al-mustaqim* (the straight path) so integral to Islam. The Dao also refers to the doctrine of the sages, which again evoked the notion of the *sunna*, or the practices of the Prophet. In this way, Muhammad and Islam were not alternatives to this tradition, but were rather inserted into it, and for the Muslim Chinese, integral to it.[26]

Although important Islamic concepts contributed to the construction of Muhammad as a sage, it is important to note that many Muslim Chinese thinkers sought to explain Muhammad's role among Chinese sages by relying primarily on Chinese texts,[27] presumably to demonstrate the ease with which Muhammad, and indeed Islam generally, could be integrated into a Confucian framework. Their reading of such texts suggested that it mattered little where a sage was from or when he lived; these were matters determined by heaven and hardly appropriate for scholarly debate.

Intent though they were to conceive of Muhammad within a Confucian worldview, most Muslim Chinese still wished to express that Muhammad was not just a sage, but an exceptional one. Liu Zhi, a prominent 18th-century Muslim writer and biographer of the Prophet, suggested a schema of different categories of saints;[28] it is clear that Muhammad and Confucius are in the most elite group, though it is (intentionally and perhaps wisely) not clear who outranked whom. Other writers were more explicit; the idea of Muhammad as 'the seal of the Prophets' (Q. 33:40) became reinterpreted as the 'completer of the Dao'. For some, this meant that the Dao was an evolving message, of which Muhammad's piece was a prominent part, and for others it meant that the Chinese Dao had been incomplete and that it required Muhammad and his message to be made whole.[29]

This effort culminated in the 18th-century collection of Chinese Islamic texts, called the *Han Kitab*, which includes several stories that in still stronger terms incorporate Muhammad into Chinese history and Confucian thought. In one such story, Muhammad saves an emperor – theoretically the highest rung of the Confucian hierarchy. In this story, therefore, the goal was not merely to insert Muhammad into the Confucian structure, but rather to place him at its pinnacle.

Venerating the Prophet Muhammad: Some Contemporary Controversies

We have explored the significance of the Prophet Muhammad for Muslims by considering some of the ways in which his devotees conceive of and relate to him: as a prophet and a statesman, as a role model and exemplar, as an intercessor and friend of the destitute, as a beloved and a lover, as a mystic blessed with the vision of God, as the perfect human, and as an avatar. In light of these multiple and varied roles it is evident why the Prophet has become the universal hallmark of identity and reverence among diverse Muslim groups. In poetry, this reverence sits frequently expressed in terms of longing for Medina, a city where Muhammad formally established the first community of believers and built the first mosque. Most importantly, when he died, he was buried there in a tomb that sits under the famed Green Dome. The poet asks,

> For how long will my heart yearn for
> Medina?
> For how long can my restless heart sigh: ah!
> Medina!
> May I die in Medina and let my grave be in
> Medina
> Carry me to my grave for I am desirous of
> Medina.[30]

It is customary for pilgrims, after they have completed the pilgrimage to Mecca, to visit Medina and pay homage to their Prophet by offering prayers at his tomb or Rawda, or 'Garden', as it is commonly called. For many pilgrims, visiting this tomb is the highlight of a lifetime and a highly emotional experience. Many recount their visit in ecstatic words, often recalling how they became tearful at their first glimpse of the Rawda. The Turkish author Emel Esin (d. 1987) captures these intense feelings:

Suddenly, he [the pilgrim] finds himself standing before the brass railing of the burial chamber itself. This place is called 'the holy countenance,' because here the visitor stands before Muhammad as he lies in his grave, his face turned towards Mecca. A round brass disc indicates the site of the Prophet's head. A vague scent of aromata pervades the air . . .

The pilgrim stands there mute. 'You must salute the Lord, salute the Lord!' whisper unknown voices behind him. But he has forgotten all that he had planned to say. Prompted by others, he tries to repeat the ancient words of the salutation: 'Peace be upon Thee, O Muhammad. I witness that Thou hast . . . ' But no sound comes from his lips. He stands there dumb and transfixed, unaware of the tears rolling down his face.[31]

To appreciate the intensity and transcendent nature of this experience, it is important to bear in mind that traditionally most Muslims consider Muhammad to be still alive spiritually in the presence of God and, as such, present whenever his devotees invoke him. In this belief they are guided by several *hadith*s, such as the following:

> The Prophet said: 'No one greets me with peace without God returning my spirit (to my body) that I may respond to this greeting of peace.'[32]

The belief in the Prophet as an enduring spiritual presence, connected intimately with the notion of the primordial Muhammadan Light, plays a significant role in popular Muslim devotional life. Thus, at the Prophet's mausoleum, while pilgrims pray to God to bless Muhammad and his family, they also beseech the Prophet for his intercession so that their sins may be forgiven and wishes fulfilled. They also fervently hope that they may be blessed by his *baraka*, a divinely bestowed beneficent force that emanates from the tomb, by touching or kissing it or the railings that surround it, or even by collecting the dust from its vicinity. Some devotees are so attuned to the Prophet's presence that they claim to have seen the Prophet's hands emerge from his tomb and bless them or hear his voice addressing them.[33] Veneration of the Prophet has also extended to relics associated with him which are believed to contain *baraka* – his mantle, sandals, weapons, staff, flag, tooth that broke in a battle, and even strands of hair.

Although veneration of the Prophet Muhammad has been widespread for centuries among Muslim communities around the world – in many of which it is considered normative – not all Muslims are comfortable with this veneration. Today, there are several Muslim groups who vehemently reject prophetic veneration as being un-Islamic, the most prominent being the so-called *muwahhidun* (monotheists), a group popularly known as the Wahhabis after their founder, Ibn Abd al-Wahhab (d. 1791). In his most famous work, *Kitab al-Tawhid* (The Book of God's Unicity), Ibn Abd al-Wahhab, citing Quranic verses and *hadith*s, describes a variety of practices that in his opinion constitute *shirk*, or associating partners with God, such as addressing intercessory prayers to others besides God and making pilgrimages to graves to seek assistance or blessing from the dead. According to him, any Muslim who believes in intercession, prays at graves, and performs other similar acts has committed heresy and is an infidel who must be fought with and killed.[34] In 1806, when the Wahhabis managed to gain control over Medina for a short while, they destroyed centuries-old tombs containing the remains of Muhammad's family and close companions, and other individuals of historic significance at al-Baqi, a vast cemetery adjacent to the Prophet's mosque. For centuries, this ancient burial ground had attracted millions of devout pilgrims who came there to pay their respects to persons they regarded as pious and partake of their *baraka*. Since Ibn Abd al-Wahhab had taught that Muhammad was an ordinary human who had left specific instructions that he did not want his grave to become a site of pilgrimage and an object of idolatry, his followers wanted to destroy the tomb of the Prophet as well. They were prevented from doing so as a result of the intervention of the Saudi ruler who needed to pacify the angry outcry from Muslims around the world. In 1925, when Wahhabi forces occupied Medina again for a longer time, they posted guards around the grave to ensure that pilgrims did not engage in any acts such as touching or kissing the tomb or prostrating before it, which they deemed polytheistic. Pilgrims caught engaged in these acts were dealt with brutally by the guards.

Such measures did not sit well with those Muslims who had espoused the long-standing traditional perspectives on issues of intercession and pilgrimage to shrines. In his Urdu travelogue, Ghulam-i Hasnain Panipati, who visited Medina in the early 1930s, severely condemns Wahhabi control over the shrines and the ill-treatment of pilgrims at the Prophet's mausoleum. Insisting on the absolute need for and legitimacy of the Prophet's intercession, he disputes the accusation that lovers of the Prophet are considered to be engaged in *shirk* or associating partners with God. He ends his description of his visit to the Prophet's tomb with a bold complaint: 'These people [the Wahhabis] have totally failed to understand the reality of Islam or the greatness of its Prophet. May God guide them.'[35]

Ironically, although Muslims may be divided about specific doctrinal issues regarding the Prophet Muhammad, belief in his prophethood continues to constitute a powerful unifying force. As expressed in the second part of the *shahada*, 'and Muhammad is His Messenger', the Prophet is central to defining Islam as a religion. Indeed, it is through Muhammad that Islam becomes crystallized as a religious system. There is a story that a Muslim claimed that his soul was so filled with the love of God that there was no room left for the love of Muhammad. The Prophet, the story claims, replied: 'He that loves God must have loved me.'[36] Whether or not this story is true, it underscores a concept with which all Muslims would agree – Muhammad's special relationship to God, his special status as God's Last Messenger, as God's Beloved, as God's Chosen One. Muhammad has remained, for centuries, a person to whom Muslims from diverse social, cultural, and denominational backgrounds could express their love and respect, their admiration, their sorrows, their joys, and their hopes. In the words of Shakeel Badayuni, the Urdu poet whom we met earlier in this chapter:

> My wish is this, that when I die I still may smile,
> And while I go, Muhammad's name be on my tongue.[37]

Chapter 3

Multisensory Religion:
Rethinking Islam

Poetry is the voice of God speaking through the lips of man. If a great painting puts you in touch with nature, great poetry puts you in direct touch with God.[1]

Millions of people around the world forge their understanding of religion through multisensory experiences. One need only walk into a church, a mosque, a temple, a synagogue, or any space of worship to experience the beauty and aesthetic power of religion to engage the senses through the arts. Every religious tradition is heavily dependent on the arts as they provide immediate ways to communicate deeply held beliefs. The arts express profound truths and emotions that are simply impossible to convey in words but must be more appropriately understood experientially. As such, an appreciation of the role of the arts is key to understanding religion as a multisensory phenomenon.

According to Muslim narratives, the religion that we today know as Islam emerged in the seventh century as an aesthetic experience that focused on encountering the Divine by listening to and being emotionally moved by the beauty of

the divine word as manifest in Quranic recitations. Since that founding moment, for the vast
majority of the world's Muslims, knowledge of
faith has been inextricably enmeshed in the
consumption and production of various arts, prin-
cipally aural, visual, and poetic arts. Hearing the
adhan (the call to prayer); reciting and listening to
the Quran; chanting the beautiful names of God;
contemplating beautifully inscribed calligraphies
or geometric designs in a mosque; singing devotional songs or poems in praise of the Prophet
Muhammad; listening to stories of the prophets;
participating in a *sama* (a concert of mystical
poetry), a *dhammal* (whirling dance), or a *muhar-
ram* assembly; venerating visual representations
of important religious personalities; taking part in
a *ta'ziya* (drama commemorating the death of
Imam Husayn) or attending a *mushaira* (a poetry
recital); singing *ginan*s; or strolling through a
paradisical garden, are just some examples of the
rich sensory repertoire through which Muslim
communities in different regions of the world
may experience varied aspects of their faith.

An approach through the arts provides us
access to expressions of Islam that are generally
not well-known as they have been marginalized
or rendered silent in the media, and in political
and social spaces. These spaces, as Mohammed
Arkoun has pointed out, are ones dominated by
what he terms 'secularized' formulations which
portray Islam as an ideology of empire building,
revivalism, identity formation, and political
legitimation articulated by competing elites.[2]

From the perspective of the cultural studies approach, the arts provide an important lens through which one can explore how Muslims interpret their faith experiences. Like religion, the arts are enmeshed in, and influenced by, an ever-evolving matrix of contexts (historical, political, economic, etc.). Historically, not only have they been a crucial way for Muslims to transmit knowledge about the faith in Muslim societies, but they have also been the vehicles through which Muslims have expressed dissent against social, political, and religious hegemonies. Notwithstanding the significant roles the arts play, it is astonishing that they have been excluded from not only public understandings of Islam but also the formal curricula about Islam in colonial and post-colonial educational systems in both Muslim and non-Muslim contexts. Representations of Islam in these contexts are predominantly textual, logocentric, visual, and historical in nature, primarily influenced by European post-Enlightenment notions of religion as a homogeneous, well-defined, and systemized ideology of identity. Such a conception cordons off and excludes the experiential multisensory aspects of the faith from consideration as religion.[3] At best, the arts are regarded as peripheral. 'The arts are the icing on the cake', a senior scholar of Islamic Studies explained to me. Another academic, commenting on a presentation I had made on the importance of understanding Islam and Muslim faith experiences through the arts, remarked: 'If I taught Islam through the arts at my university, it would not be tolerated; I would be laughed out of the room.'

The Quran and the Arts

Muslim narratives about the centrality of the arts in faith experiences are rooted in the Quran, the scripture at the heart of Islam. Although today the Quran is popularly conceived of as a physical book, a written scripture, during Muhammad's lifetime it was primarily a performative text that was recited, heard, and experienced – hence its name 'Quran', meaning 'Recitation'. In other words, it functioned as an aural/oral scripture.[4] The experiential nature of the Quran is evident in Muslim historiographical accounts of the scripture's first revelation to Muhammad. According to these accounts, Muhammad used to retreat regularly to a small cave atop Mount Hira on the outskirts of Mecca where he would meditate. On one such visit, while he was in contemplation, he heard a voice commanding, 'Recite!' Terrified, he responded, 'I am not a reciter!' However, the voice repeated the command, and once again he responded he was not a reciter. The third time he heard the voice, he felt as if he was being held in such a tight embrace that he gasped for breath. Eventually, he found himself reciting the following verse, the words of which he claimed were inscribed on his heart:

Recite in the name of Your Lord who created!
Who created the human from a clot of blood.

Recite: and your Lord is the Most Bountiful
Who has taught by the Pen
Taught the human what they did not know.
(Q. 96:1–5)

As presented in accounts of Muhammad's life, this experience constituted his first encounter with the ineffable, the transcendent God, the booming voice being attributed to the Angel Gabriel, the Holy Spirit, through which the Divine revealed itself to humankind. It was an experience during which Muhammad was totally overwhelmed by divine majesty (*jalal*), one that left him shaken to the core of his very being. An experience in which one encounters the terrifying otherness of God is present in many religious traditions, as Rudolf Otto demonstrates in *The Idea of the Holy*.[5] It is described as the *mysterium tremendum*, the 'overwhelming mystery'. In Hebrew it is referred to simply as *kaddosh* (holiness).[6]

Trembling and shivering, Muhammad fled the cave and ran home where his beloved wife, Khadija, comforted him. She covered him with a shawl and assured him that he was not possessed by a *jinn* (spirit). She also assured him that he was a prophet. For the next two decades, Muhammad continued receiving these revelations which would overwhelm him, but as he recited them aloud, they came to be called *qur'an*s (recitations). The symbols, metaphors, sound patterns, as well as the poetic and linguistic structure of these recitations resonated

deeply with a pre-Islamic Arab cultural context
in which the poetic arts and beauty of expression
were highly prized. Consequently, Muhammad's
audiences possessed 'the most finely honed and
scrutinizing tastes in the history of expressive
speech'.[7] People flocked to hear Muhammad's
recitations, claiming they had never heard
anything more beautiful in the Arabic language.
To paraphrase a Quranic verse, the most beautiful of recitations caused the skin of listeners to
shiver and their hearts to melt.[8] Many were so
deeply affected by the beauty of the text that they
would weep openly and uncontrollably.[9] Indeed,
a few accounts narrate that Muhammad's most
bitter enemies broke down in tears after listening
to a recitation and became adherents.[10] In this
regard, Muslim narratives particularly highlight
the sudden 'conversion' of Umar b. al-Khattab
(d. 644), a critic and enemy of Muhammad, who
became Muhammad's disciple after his heart
was 'softened' by the mesmerizing beauty of a
recitation of some Quranic verses which had
reduced him to tears.[11]

The impact of the Quranic recitations on
audiences was such that an informal community
of listeners rapidly formed around Muhammad
in Mecca. However, some detractors considered
him to be a magician or a sorcerer; others
accused him of being a poet, for, in pre-Islamic
Arabian society, words recited by poets were
conceived to have a powerful spiritual potency
as they were believed to be inspired by *jinns*.[12]
Muhammad responded by declaring that he was

a prophet who received revelation from the One Almighty God. In response to demands for proof of this claim, he challenged sceptics to produce a text matching the beauty of the Quranic verses, boldly asserting that no human or *jinn* could create a text like it.[13] In this way, the beauty of the Quranic recitations became proof of their divine origin. Unsurprisingly, Muslim narratives do not attribute the success of Muhammad's mission and the spread of the faith to sociopolitical or economic factors, but rather to the literary and aesthetic qualities of the Quran, a text whose beauty no one could resist. In this regard, the contemporary Iranian scholar, Muhammad Taqi Shariati-Mazinani, comments:

> The Arab, already besotted with the beauty of language, suddenly heard an oration like none he had ever heard before . . . he thrilled to this oratory and was enraptured, he was amazed and astonished, it transformed, changed and delighted him. The Quran's words fell like rays of light on him; the listener found himself immersed in light; it enveloped his whole being and every particle of his existence, illuminating his heart and mind. The Quran was a light that shone into the soul through the aperture of the ear; it transformed the soul, and as a result, the world.[14]

Indeed, the experiential dimension of the Quran extends beyond the aural/oral to the visual. Many verses of the Quran instruct believers to look around them, as they are surrounded by the Face of God; the signs of God are manifest in nature, with all of creation glorifying the Divine, if only we could 'hear' and 'see' correctly:

> The seven heavens and the earth and everyone in them glorify Him. There is not a single thing that does not glorify Him with praise but you do not understand their praise.
>
> (Q. 17:44)

> Do you not see that all those who are in the heavens and the earth praise God, as do the birds with wings outstretched? Each knows its [own way] of prayer and glorification: God has full knowledge of what they do.
>
> (Q. 24:41)

The notion that beauty is a manifestation of the Divine inspired the notion of the 99 'beautiful names' (asma al-husna) of God, as well as the famous saying attributed to the Prophet Muhammad, 'God is beautiful and loves beauty.' All beauty in the world came to be seen as a reflection or symbol of God's beauty and as something that can, therefore, potentially be a transformative force on the soul. Through engagement with beauty, it is believed that one can attain the highest dimension of faith, ihsan (meaning, 'to do things beautifully'), and become a beautiful person, muhsin (one who mirrors or reflects God's beauty). Theologically speaking, then, 'indifference to beauty is tantamount to indifference to God'.[15]

Demonstrating a particularly acute sensitivity to the beauty of Quranic recitations were the esoterically inclined Sufis who longed to 'experience' the Divine as the Prophet Muhammad had during the *mi'raj*, or his celestial journey. For them, listening (*sama*) to Quranic recitation was a means by which they could experience the sacred. Sufi lore is replete with examples of individuals who responded to Quranic recitations by entering an ecstatic state, or *wajd* (finding, or connecting). As a result, they would weep and fall into states of rapture with uncontrolled body movements, or collapse unconscious. During this intense experience, they are said to have had a taste (*dhawq*) of the Divine. According to many accounts, some Sufis were so completely overcome by the experience that they died. Notable in this regard is Abu Ishaq al-Tha'labi's *Book of Those Slain by the Noble Quran, Who Heard the Quran and Died Thereupon* which records 19 such cases.[16]

Beautifying the Spoken Word

Through the centuries, listening to the Quran has continued to be an important means through which individuals would commune with the Divine and experience spiritual peace and tranquillity (*sakina*). To actualize this communion, the Quranic text needs to be activated through melody and performance. As

Kristina Nelson aptly describes it, 'melody is the means by which the divine is comprehended. At that point great art happens.'[17] Elaborating on this point, Navid Kermani writes:

> If one follows the rules for an ideal recita-
> tion as outlined by Sufi authors such as al-
> Ghazali and al-Makki, the musical rendition
> is not only 'ornament' in the ordinary sense
> of the term – an element that is pleasing but
> ultimately extrinsic to the understanding
> of the essential part, the content – on the
> contrary, it is basic to the actualization of the
> message. All the Muslim doctrines of Quran
> recitation suggest that it should be a compre-
> hensive religious experience that touches the
> senses, the mind and the spirit. It should not
> be the mere transmission of information or,
> of course, the opposite, pure entertainment.[18]

Thus, to be effective, it is incumbent upon the reciter (*qari*) to recite the text in a manner that touches both their own heart and the hearts of listeners. In the words of Abdul Basit Abdus Samad (d. 1988), the renowned Egyptian reciter, 'the Quran, when recited from the heart, reaches the heart'.[19]

Muhammad himself, who is renowned in communal memory for the beauty of his recita-tions, encouraged his followers to make the same efforts in their own recitations: 'Embellish the Quran with your voices, for a beautiful voice increases the beauty of the Quran.'[20] Such injunctions seem to have been interpreted quite liberally in the early period (seventh and eighth centuries), with some reciters using melodies from popular poems and songs to sing the Quran. These developments, as well as concerns about the clarity of the message of the text being distorted or overwhelmed by melody, led to the development of a code, *tajwid*, that regulated Quran recitation. To qualify as a reciter, one had to be rigorously trained and have knowledge of many details such as lengthening and shortening vowels, being aware of places where pausing during recitation was permissible or forbidden, nasalization, as well as the etiquette of recitation.[21] Over time, two styles evolved – the *murratal* style and the *mujawwad* style. The *murratal* style involves straight recitation of the text in a sing-song manner, strictly according to the rules of *tajwid*. Commonly used for prayers and devotional practices, its impact on listeners has been described as soothing, restful, refreshing, and hypnotic. In contrast, the *mujawwad* style, used in formal public performances, interprets the text with much more artistry in order to reach 'the heart of listeners'. It is characterized by elaborate vocal embellishments, and by repetitions of words and/or phrases with meaningful pauses during which the audience expresses their emotions through rapturous moaning, weeping, or ecstatic exclamations such as 'Allah! Allah!'

There are several modes of 'officially' approved recitations, each with their unique characteristics. Maria Ulfah, one of the most

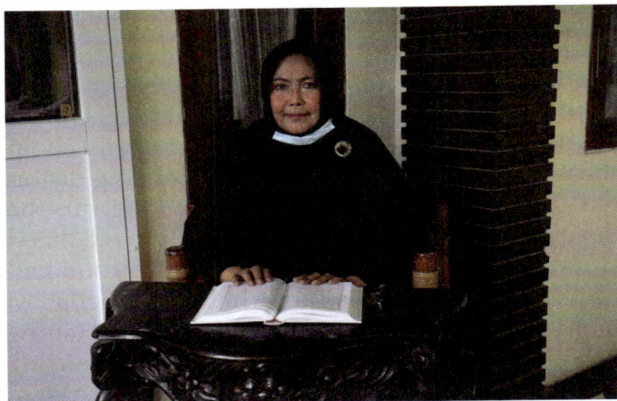

Figure 12. Maria Ulfah
Here, the prominent Quran reciter poses for a portrait at the Baitul Qurro Islamic
Boarding School where she teaches Quran recitation in Jakarta, Indonesia.

influential and popular female Quran reciters in
all of Southeast Asia, explains that the reciter
must understand the meaning of what is being
recited and match the recitation to it:

> One might use a regal mode for passages that
> reveal God's laws, and a more sensitive or
> quiet mode for passages that relate to personal
> spirituality. One mode might suit public
> competitions, weddings or other celebrations
> – such as *mujawwad*, the most melodic and
> popular style – while another would better
> suit recitation at home.[22]

Today, Quran recitation has developed into such
a highly developed art form that every year

thousands of Muslims from around the world gather to participate in local, national, and international Quran recitation competitions with the most outstanding reciters being recognized with cash prizes and high status in society. When Maria Ulfah was asked whether such competitions interfere with religious understanding, she responded:

> The tradition of *musabaqat tilawat al-Qur'an* [Quran recitation contests] arises genuinely from the teachings of Islam, which urge Muslims to read and learn the Qur'an in order to be able understand and practice their religion properly. Every Muslim is expected to be able to read the Qur'an, at least in a simple manner for the purpose of performing prayers.
>
> There are, however, children and young people who are blessed with good voices . . . They understandably pursue further the study of the techniques of recitation of the Qur'an.[23]

As part of their religious education, nearly all Muslims memorize and learn to recite verses of the Quran, especially those used during prayer. Those who memorize the entire text are honoured with the title *hafiz al-Quran* (keeper or protector of the Quran). As Michael Sells remarks, beyond rote memorization, they are also 'interiorizing the inner rhythms, sound patterns, and textual dynamics – taking it to heart in the deepest manner'.[24] Indeed, in certain parts of West Africa, schooling around the Quran adopts a holistic approach: it seeks to mould the entire person so as to reshape them as living embodiments of the Quranic message. As was the case with the Prophet Muhammad, they become 'walking Qurans', exemplary embodiments of God's Word.[25]

Today, Muslims encounter the recited Quran in a vast array of contexts beyond spaces of formal worship and performance. Recitations are heard in shops and crowded bazars, and even in the streets recited by beggars. There are recitations at the beginning of public events; in taxis, trains, and airplanes; on the radio, television, and Internet.[26] In these, and in many other ways, the Quran is at the heart of an Islamic soundscape that permeates traditions of spirituality and the arts of calligraphy, poetry, music, and dance. All these serve as vehicles to help individuals transcend the material and the physical and experience the spiritual.

Calligraphy: Beautifying the Written Word

After the death of the Prophet Muhammad, the orally transmitted recitations, along with bits and pieces which had been recorded on various materials, were collated into a single authorized scripture (*mushaf*) as part of a state-sponsored project that made the Quranic text a pre-text for the emergent Umayyad state.[27] In a society in which the majority were illiterate, the compilation of a fixed codex privileged written culture over oral culture, eventually leading to the emergence of a class of scholars (*ulama*) who claimed authority to interpret the text based on the knowledge they had acquired through their formal study.[28] In this way, the written text of the Quran became the basis for a variety of ideological (legalistic, philosophical, spiritualistic) formulations of Islam. It is also significant to note that when copies of the first written versions of the Quran were initially distributed, they were always accompanied by a reciter, emphasizing the continuing importance of the aural/oral over the written, a supremacy that still prevails today, particularly in devotional contexts.

Just as the Quran needs to be melodiously recited so that it moves the heart, it also had to be beautifully written to please the eye. Calligraphy, from the Greek words *kallos* (beauty) and *graphein* (to write), meaning 'the art of beautiful writing', has been described as music for the eyes as well as 'the art of making words sing'.[29] Arabic calligraphy has been highly honoured and esteemed, diligently developed and practised as an important religious art form by Muslims the world over. The special significance attached to calligraphy stems from the central role that writing plays in Islamic thought. Islam is the first religion to have made the distinction between people who have received a written form of revelation (*ahl al-kitab*) and those who have not. Several verses of the Quran accord a great deal of importance to writing due to its connection with knowledge. For instance, the first chapter to be revealed, *Surat al-Alaq* (Q. 96), emphasizes that God taught humans what they did not know, by the Pen, while *Surat al-Qalam* (Q. 68) begins with the words, '*Nun* and by the Pen!' – words that have been interpreted by some commentators as an allusion to the exalted status of writing. Furthermore, the Quran refers to the *lawh al-mahfuz* (the Well-Preserved Tablet) or the *umm al-kitab* (the Mother of the Book), which is the heavenly prototype of all earthly scriptures on which everything from eternity has been written by the Celestial Pen.[30] It also speaks about the *kiram al-katibin* (noble scribe angels), who sit on a person's shoulders recording their every action. As a result of such references, writing came to be seen as having a divine or otherworldly origin, giving rise to the idea in many Islamic languages that each person's destiny (*maktub*[31] in Arabic, literally, 'that which has been written') is 'written' on the face, particularly on the forehead.[32] The Prophet Muhammad, too, gave importance to writing when he had the early Muslims record the Quranic recitations on materials such as leather parchment and the shoulder blades of sheep. Furthermore, according to a *hadith*, Muhammad is believed to have said, '"He who writes the *bismillah* beautifully obtains innumerable blessings" or "will enter paradise".'[33]

Copying the Quran was a pious act in which all Muslims, ranging from rulers to the most humble devotee, could engage. However, professional calligraphers enjoyed a special importance in Muslim societies. Popular legend had it that, because they wrote God's word, calligraphers were destined to go to paradise. Furthermore, since the Quran can be touched or recited only in a state of ritual purity, calligraphers had to be physically and spiritually pure in order that they may be worthy of writing the Quran. Calligraphers were required to be morally impeccable, modest, and hardworking, and always had to practise lest they lose their skill. Becoming a calligrapher was a long and arduous task that required, as in most branches of Islamic learning, the interested person to find a master to provide instruction and supervision during the constant rehearsing of letters of the script. Sound knowledge of writing implements was also a requirement.[34]

The conception of the aural Quran as a manifestation of Divine Beauty also contributed significantly to the importance of calligraphy as 'the external dress' for the invisible Word of God in the visible world. Thus, as visual embodiments of the Divine Word, the letters had to be written in the most beautiful manner, befitting their special status.[35] As visible manifestations of spiritual realities, the letters were also regarded as sacred, possessing special power (*baraka*) to act as talismans to protect against evil or harm. Thus, in many Muslim cultures, Quranic verses engraved on bracelets and pendants are widely used as amulets for healing and protection. Similarly, miniature copies of

Figure 13. Seal Ring with Inscription
Carved on the surface is the Nad-i Ali, an invocation to Ali, the Prophet's cousin.
Dated to the late 15th or early 16th century, from Iran or Central Asia.

Figure 14. Miniature Quran
Very fine calligraphic script has been inscribed in Qurans such as these.

Qurans contained in tiny boxes are often hung
in homes as well as in different modes of trans-
port to provide a layer of divine safety for
the occupants.

The earliest calligraphers were primarily
focused on the text of the Quran. It was first
written in a somewhat slanting style in a script
known as *ma'il* and then in a more angular style
known as *kufic*, since it originated in the city of
Kufa. Tradition considers Ali b. Abi Talib, the

Prophet's son-in-law, to be the first calligrapher in the *kufic* style and ascribes to him the invention of certain types of Kufic letters. Most calligraphers, in fact, traced their pedigree to Imam Ali. These early forms of Arabic calligraphy lacked diacritics and, therefore, readers would have to apply their prior knowledge of the memorized text in order to read it correctly. For more secular purposes, such as administrative record-keeping, normal correspondence, and the copying of books, a cursive rounded and easy to write style was used, which later developed into the *naskh* style. After 751, when Muslims became acquainted with the manufacture of paper – a cheaper and lighter material than the parchment or papyrus that were then in use – more elegant writing styles emerged. By the 10th

Figure 15a. Architectural Calligraphy
Museum of the Future, Dubai, UAE, with its façade of stainless steel and its windows forming an Arabic poem.

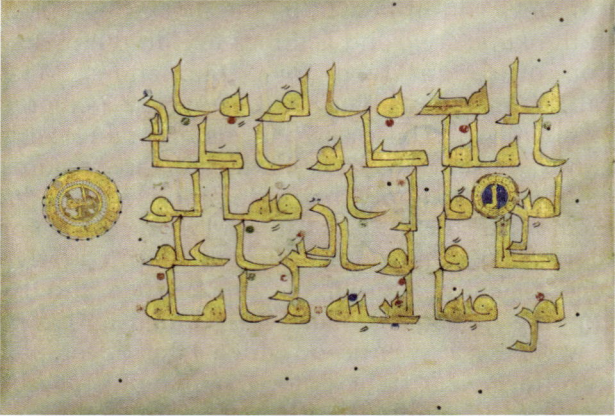

Figure 15b. Quran Leaf with Kufic Script
The calligraphy here appears in gold ink; the page is taken from a Quran dated to the 900s.

Figure 15c. Islamic 'Calligraffiti'
Islamic calligraphy on a wall on a street of Chattogram, Bangladesh.

Figure 15d. Turkish Prayer Rug
Turkish prayer rug with legible inscription at its borders and pseudo-Kufic writing at the foot, ca. 17th century.

Figure 15e. Calligraphy Showing Some Names of Allah
Oil painting by Ayeza Nadeem showing some of the names of God.

Figure 15f. 'Calligraffiti', London
Calligraffiti by the French-Tunisian artist eL Seed painted on a wall in Shoreditch, London.

century, there seemed to have been at least 12 styles of calligraphy in use, with as many variations. However, master calligraphers such as Ibn Muqla (d. 940), Ibn al-Bawwab (d. 1022), and Yaqut al-Musta'simi (d. 1298) codified the art of calligraphy outlining the scientific rules for beautiful writing by using circular and straight lines and rhombic points that gave the letters the correct size and shape. Six disciples of Yaqut are credited with inventing the *aqlam al-sitta*, the six major styles which remained in use throughout the centuries: *naskh*, *rihani*, *muhaqqaq*, *tawqi*, *riqa*, and *thuluth*. With the establishment of these six basic styles, the multiplicity of earlier styles fell into oblivion.[36] However, distinctive calligraphic styles did emerge in regional contexts such as Spain, North Africa, India, Iran, and China, which reflected local tastes. In China, for example, a unique style of Arabic calligraphy emerged that employed Chinese techniques, such as using a brush rather than the reed pen to write Arabic letters. The central role that the calligraphic arts have played in Islamic religious life resulted in the Arabic script becoming a badge of identity for Muslim peoples all over the world. The script and the calligraphic tradition associated with it served as a unifying factor within the linguistically and culturally diverse community. More importantly, the Arabic script commonly known as the *huruf al-Quran* (the letters of the Quran) was considered to be the most precious treasure for Muslims and was adapted to write almost all the languages of the

Islamic world including Persian, Urdu, Sindhi, Hausa, and Swahili, to name just a few. Within the corpus of religious literature, calligraphy was by no means confined to copying the Quran: the *asma al-husna* (the 99 beautiful names of God), the *hadith*, beautiful renderings of pious phrases such as *bismillah*, *al-hamdulillah*, *mashallah*, and in the Shiʻi environment the names of Ali b. Abi Talib and other Shiʻi imams, all became themes for elegant calligraphic compositions. Calligraphy made its appearance on a wide variety of everyday objects that included coins, eating and drinking vessels, weapons, jewellery, and textiles. A great deal of the charm of Islamic calligraphy stems from the freedom, flow, and elasticity that the Arabic script offers the artist. Manipulating the flexibility of the script, a skilful calligrapher is able to create an infinite number of designs from one letter or even a word. Thus, the *nad-i aliyyan* (the invocation to Ali b. Abi Talib, the first Shiʻi Imam) was frequently written in the shape of a lion representative of his epithet 'The Lion of God', or the phrase *bismillah* (In the name of God) could be written as a bird, or the *shahada* (the confession of the faith) could be formed into a boat of salvation carrying the faithful to the shore of paradise. These calligraphic designs had such universal appeal and charm that we find imitations of Arabic calligraphy occurring in the decoration of churches and shrines in medieval Italy, Spain, and France. As a result, verses of the Quran written in calligraphy even appear on church walls.

A distinctive aspect of Arabic calligraphy is its extensive use on the external and internal facades of buildings. Quranic verses, assorted religious phrases of benediction and supplication, and verses of poetry were used to adorn and sanctify mosques, madrasas, and mausoleums. The significance of these inscriptions can be interpreted from several perspectives and can vary from monument to monument. A particularly interesting example of such usage is the Taj Mahal, one of the architectural wonders of the world. Built by the Mughal emperor Shah Jahan (d. 1666) as a mausoleum and monument to love for his beloved wife Mumtaz Mahal (d. 1631), the entire complex is set in a quadripartite garden with a long reflecting pool. It was inspired by Quranic notions of paradise – attempting to capture what it would feel like to be in the presence of God – through the metaphor of a peaceful and beautiful garden filled with multisensory experiences such as the sound of flowing rivers and the smell of the surrounding fragrant flowers and trees. The octagonal marble lattice screen encircling the cenotaphs of Mumtaz Mahal and Shah Jahan is richly decorated with inlay work of precious stones representing flowers and leaves executed so perfectly that they look almost real. In this sense, the mausoleum-garden complex in which Mumtaz Mahal and, later Shah Jahan, were laid to rest was intended to provide an anticipatory glimpse into the invisible world beyond. For the complex, Shah Jahan, in collaboration with his calligrapher, Amanat Khan, chose 241 Quranic verses selected from 25 chapters, for a vast inscriptional programme, the likes of which had never been seen in Mughal India.[37] The texts were beautifully inscribed in marble with inlay work both inside and outside the mausoleum as well as at the doorways and central gateway. After 'reading' this monument through its Quranic inscriptions, Michael Calabria, an expert on Arabic literature, concludes that the mausoleum is just as much an exquisite monument of love as it is a statement of Shah Jahan's interpretation of his Muslim faith, embedded within the discourse of beauty:

> In addition to being an elegant expression of Shah Jahan's love, the Taj Mahal is also an eloquent testimony to his Islamic faith, a faith he approached sincerely but lived imperfectly. The Taj Mahal is, in essence, Shah Jahan's Qur'an, proclaiming the most salient teachings of Islam in a realm that was religiously and culturally diverse . . . By rendering the surahs of the Qur'an in monumental form, Shah Jahan and his calligrapher Amanat Khan gave the texts a highly visible presence in the world beyond the page of the handwritten volume . . . The inscriptions serve as a visual representation of God's eternal word revealed to humanity. Their very presence in this form, in the language of their revelation, makes them true, real, and meaningful – for the living and the dead.[38]

Seen as a tangible expression of Shah Jahan's Quran, the Taj Mahal thus lies at the heart of an

Islamic landscape, or perhaps, more accurately, an 'artscape' focused on experiencing the invisible world through the visible and through 'tasting' (*dhawq*) or experiencing the transcendent.

Poetic Arts

In his epic poem, *Javid-nama*, Sir Muhammad Iqbal writes: 'If the purpose of poetry is the fashioning of men, poetry is likewise the heir of prophecy.'[39] These lines from one of the most important Muslim poet-philosophers of the 20th century reflect well the central and transformative role that poets, as heirs of the Prophet, have played in shaping Muslim societies. To understand how poetry and poets have come to hold such a distinctive role, we need to turn to the Quran and its emergence in the seventh century within a

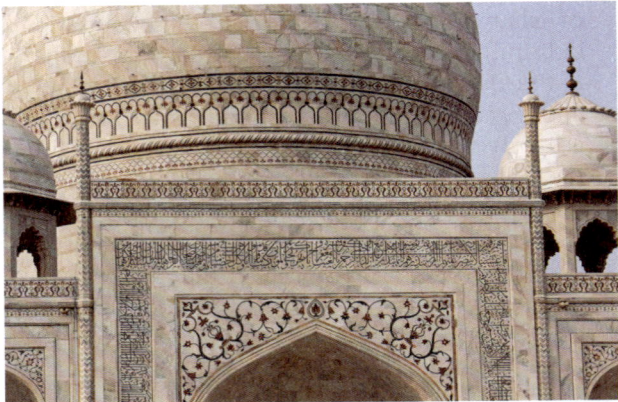

Figure 15g. Calligraphy on the Taj Mahal
Inscription detail from the Taj Mahal, India.

Figure 15h. The *Basmala* in the *Sini* Style of Calligraphy

The *Sini* style combines traditional Arabic calligraphy with the characteristic features of Chinese brushwork.

culture where poetic arts and the beauty of oral expression were most highly prized and esteemed. In an environment in which audiences had developed refined and discerning tastes,[40] poets played not only a prominent role but a critical one as well. They were not merely word artists, but, through their compositions, they served as oral historians, journalists, and publicists all rolled into one. They also defended the honour of their tribes. It was customary to recognize talented poets by having their compositions embroidered in gold and hung from the walls of the Ka'ba, an important pilgrimage centre in pre-Islamic Arabia. While poets were revered and acclaimed, they were also feared due to their extraordinary knowledge, popularly considered to be inspired by *jinns* (spirits). Hence, their words were endowed with spiritual and magical potency. This power was particularly apparent in satirical poetry in which the poet employed exquisitely crafted language filled with innuendo to attack the tribe's enemies, thus destroying their reputation through ridicule, contempt, and denigration. These 'curses in verses' were dreaded by their intended victims since, unlike physical wounds inflicted on a body by arrows or swords which could potentially be healed, poetic 'wounds' inflicted on an enemy's honour would be fatal to one's reputation since they would be remembered through poetic transmission for many generations to come.

Given this context, it is hardly surprising that when Muhammad began reciting beautifully composed verses that eventually came to be compiled into the Quran, he was immediately accused by his opponents of being a poet or a soothsayer. Responding to such accusations, he clarified that he was a prophet, distinguishing a poet who is driven by egotistical desires (see, for example, *Surat al-Shu'ara* – Q. 26) from a prophet who utters the truth that is revealed by the one God. Although the Quran was critical of poets, acute sensibility to the spoken word, its aesthetic qualities, as well as ethical values espoused in pre-Islamic Arabic poetry (such as generosity, bravery, hospitality) became characteristic of the Quranic discourse, albeit in a new religious framework. Poets regarded Muhammad as a rival competing for audiences; thus they ranked among his most bitter opponents. When one of them, Ka'b, son of the renowned poet Zuhayr, eventually pledged allegiance to the Prophet, he did so by presenting Muhammad with a *qasida* (praise poem) he had specially composed to honour him. Moved by the eloquence of this poetic gift, Muhammad took off his *burda* (cloak) and placed it around Ka'b's shoulders. Henceforth, the poem came to be known as the 'Burda' or 'Mantle Ode'. It was the first example of a new genre of poetry in praise of the Prophet that was to become ubiquitous in all Islamic literatures. This transaction between the poet and the Prophet marks, simultaneously, the rejection of some pre-Islamic values and the transformation of other values in the new religious worldview heralded with the coming of Islam. Subsequently, as Michael Sells points out, instead of being draped with the odes of pre-Islamic poets, the Ka'ba became adorned with a black cloth embroidered with verses from the Quran.[41] More importantly, poetry, once shunned for representing the ideals of paganism, was brought into the service of Islam.

The tradition that began with pre-Islamic poetry continued to develop through the history of Arabic and other Islamic literatures. Muslim poets adapted the pre-Islamic genre of the *qasida* (the monorhyme praise poem) for religious purposes. In addition to praising a ruler or a poet's patron, the *qasida* was now also used to praise God, to eulogize the Prophet, or to laud or lament the martyr heroes of Shi'i Islam. In the ninth century, as traditions of Islamic love mysticism emerged, prominent mystics such as Rabi'a al-Adawiya (d. 801), Dhu'l-Nun (d. 859), al-Hallaj (d. 922), and Ibn al-Farid (d. 1235) composed mystical love poetry in Arabic, drawing upon the *qasida*'s amatory prelude, the *nasib*. Its themes of remembering and longing for a lost beloved exquisitely conveyed the many aspects and phases of the mystics' relationship with the Divine Beloved – the anguish of separation, the blissful reunion, the endless striving to be worthy and faithful, and the yearning and longing for spiritual union with the Divine. Among these, Rabi'a became the focus of many legends.[42] According to the most popular, she was once seen roaming the streets of Basra (in present-day Iraq) with a torch in one hand and a pitcher of water in the other, declaring that she was looking for paradise so that with the fire of the torch she could burn it, and that she was also looking for hell so that with the water from the pitcher she could extinguish its fires. When asked why she wanted to destroy paradise and extinguish the fires of hell, she responded: 'Because people worship God either out of hope [of going to paradise] or out of fear [of being cast into hell].' In her view, worshipping God out of hope or fear was selfish, for it was concerned ultimately with the preservation of self. True worship of God needs to be God-centric not self-centric. Importantly, it needs to be based on unconditional love without any expectation or ulterior motive. In one of the many verses attributed to her, she declares:

O Lord, if I worship You out of fear of hell,
    burn me in hell.
If I worship [You] in the hope of [paradise],
    forbid it to me.
But if I worship You for Your own sake,
Do not deprive me of Your [eternal] beauty.[43]

Many verses from this growing corpus of mystically themed poetry began to be sung accompanied by instruments in the *sama* (musical concerts of poetry). The ecstatic response of listeners to these poetic verses was reminiscent of listeners' responses to the Quran.

It was in the 13th century that Arabic poetry became overshadowed by the dramatic rise and popularity of poetry in Persian across Iran and Central and South Asia. This produced some of the world's greatest mystic poets such as Rumi, Hafiz, and Attar. The symbols, metaphors, and imagery associated with intoxicating love and longing for the elusive beloved in their poetic compositions were regarded as creative expressions informed by their mystical experiences. In the case of Rumi, his biographer, Dawlatshah, records that when he was in an ecstatic state, 'drowned in the ocean of love', he would take hold of a pillar in his house and set himself turning around it, reciting verses which his disciples would write down.[44] This kind of divine/spiritual inspiration bestowed on poets was called *ilham* in order to distinguish it from *wahy*, the inspiration received by prophets. As a result, compositions such as the *Mathnawi-yi ma'anawi* of Rumi and the *Diwan* of Hafiz came to be regarded as texts that provide Persian speakers with access to the inner or esoteric (*batin*) meaning of the Arabic Quran in their own language. In recognition of its intermediary 'scriptural' role, the *Mathanawi* of Rumi came to be called 'the Quran in Persian' while Hafiz was given the epithet 'Tongue of the

Hidden'. Like all poetic texts, these compositions of religious mysticism were intended to be sung in appropriate musical modes and accompanied by musical instrumentation during the *sama* with the goal of giving rise to an ecstatic state among listeners. In this manner, poetry that was a product of one individual's spiritual experience became, through performance, the source of inspiration for another's experience.

Over time, these poets were acclaimed as *awliya* (friends of God, or saints) – individuals who were close to God – and their tomb-shrines (*dargah*s) became sites of pilgrimage where devotees could seek their blessings. That these ancient poets continue to be venerated in contemporary Iran is best captured by Patricia Almarcegui in the following quote:

> The mausoleums of the poets, open from eight in the morning to eleven in the evening, are full of Iranians. Omar [Kh]ayyam's and Farid U[d]-Din Attar's in Nishapur, Ferdusi's in Tus, Al-Saadi's and Hafez's in Shiraz, etc. Iranians from all parts of the country go there to recite verses of the poets, to remember them with music, to walk in couples, to eat or drink, to sing their poems together as a family, to see the moon and reflect on life and death.[45]

Beyond the Arabo-Persian world, poetic arts flourished in other regions as well. For example, for centuries, poets have played a central role in shaping ethical, moral, philosophical, and spiritual life in South Asia. Poetry is popularly referred to as *ruh ki giza* (food for the soul). The knowledge that poetic traditions embody and convey in diverse languages is not only discursive but is also meant to be felt or experienced through performance. Hence, Nosheen Ali has aptly referred to it as *mannkahat* ('heart–mind' knowledge).[46] Like their Persian counterparts, many of these poets are also regarded as friends of God, attracting thousands to their tomb-shrines seeking not only spiritual edification but also blessings for the alleviation of difficulties and the fulfilment of wishes.

We can cite, by way of example, the highly acclaimed poet Shah Abdul Latif (d. 1752), whose mausoleum at Bhit in Sindh is visited every day by thousands of pilgrims who come to pay their respects to the one whom they consider a *pir* (spiritual guide). He is renowned for the masterful way in which he represents in his magnum opus, the *Risalo*, the numerous heroines (*surmis*) of popular Sindhi folk romances. These he portrays as symbols of the soul, each heroine longing for union with her beloved (God). Considered to be one of the most revered texts of Sindhi literature, the *Risalo*'s 30 chapters are framed around popular folktales, each meant to be sung in a distinctive melody. To this day, a group of specially trained *faqir*s sing selections from the *Risalo* at his shrine at Bhit in falsetto in order to imitate the voices of his heroines.[47] Shah Abdul Latif does not tell stories in their entirety, assuming that audiences are familiar with the plots. Instead, he focuses on representing the thoughts and feelings of the heroines at dramatic points in the plot. Through the deft use of exegetical remarks, he then interprets these thoughts to explain various stages and states of the mystical journey of the soul, often drawing on Quranic verses and/or *hadith*s. Clearly, he perceives the function of his poetry to be much more than mere narrative. In this regard, he writes:

> Think not . . . that these are mere couplets,
>   they are signs . . .
> They bear thee to thy True Friend, and have
>   inspired thee with true love.[48]

In contemporary South Asia, these poetic traditions continue to flourish in various genres

Figure 16. Abida Parveen
Abida Parveen in performance in Oslo, 2007.

such as women's work songs, lullabies, and mystical romances. Particularly popular is the *qawwali*, a uniquely South Asian genre that originated from the *sama* rituals performed at Sufi shrines, in which poetry composed in various languages is sung to north Indian *raga*s or melodies, and *tal*s or beats. As devotional music, *qawwali* highlights singing as an act of worship and transcendence, a characteristic that it shares with other South Asian genres such as *bhajan*s and *kirtan*s, the devotional hymns associated with the region's Hindu and Sikh communities respectively. Notable here is the contribution of Abida Parveen (b. 1954), the eminent singer of Punjabi and Sindhi Sufi poetry, who has successfully promoted and popularized local or regional genres such as the *qawwali* and *sufiana kalam* on the world music stage.

* * *

Here we have explored the central role that the Quran plays at the heart of an Islamic 'artscape', one that provides opportunities to experience the beauty of the transcendent through the aural arts (Quranic and poetic recitation, *dhikr*, *sama*), the visual arts (calligraphy, architecture, painting), and the poetic arts. Exploring Islam through the lens of this artscape enables us to encounter, and indeed experience, faith perspectives that have often been overshadowed, marginalized, and, in some instances, silenced by the voices of 'loud' Islam that have come to dominate the media, and political and social spaces today.

This artscape also challenges notions of what constitutes religion. These, as we have pointed out previously, have been shaped by post-Enlightenment European notions embedded in discourses of colonialism and nationalism, conceiving of religion as an ideology of identity, often posited against the 'other'. Such notions have proven to be toxic today and are responsible for conflicts in so many parts of the world. Approaching religion through the arts humanizes what has been dehumanized by contemporary political discourses. Furthermore, it questions notions in Western academia that imagine a strict divide between religion and art. It compels us to ask questions such as: What does it mean to call some art religious? How can interpreting an individual believer's engagement with the arts help us see religion in a new light? Our responses to these questions would centre on the diverse local Muslim communities across the world and the varied contexts in which they experience their faith. Approaching Islam through the arts ultimately represents an 'Islam with conceptual cohesion underlying diverse material and ethereal manifestations. Above and beyond enhancing our understanding of an Islamic other, it can enable the sharing of ideas across times and cultures, enriching the possibilities through which we moderns apprehend our world.'[49]

Conclusion

When we hear a news story about religious conflict or coexistence, it is easy to retreat to simplistic and even exaggerated claims about what this or that religion espouses. How do we get past reductive descriptions of religion? When confronted with conflicting information about a religion, how do we make sense of these competing claims?

From the perspective of the cultural studies approach that anchors this book, we have seen that, although some may regard religions to be divinely revealed, their meanings are humanly constructed and constantly being reshaped. As a result, all religious traditions are marked by diversity and change. Like any other religion, Islam is marked by diversity. There are many interpretations of Islam and what it means to be Muslim, each shaped by its own context. There are also different discourses through which these interpretations can be expressed, from the theological, the legal, and the scriptural to the artistic and the poetic.

We have also remarked, time and again, that religions are ultimately cultural phenomena and do not themselves have agency. Although many people tend to personify religions ('Islam says', etc.), religions do not, and indeed cannot, say or do anything since they are abstract concepts. As such, they are neither intrinsically good nor bad, violent nor peaceful. Rather, it is the adherents of a particular religion who interpret its ideas and beliefs to justify a wide range of political, social, and cultural goals conditioned by the realities of their lives.

As a result, religious traditions are polyvalent and marked by contradiction. Some Muslims, based on their interpretation of Quranic verses, emphasize the *jamal*, the beautiful and loving aspect of the Divine. They relate to God through love, the intoxicating and self-transforming love for a divine beloved whom they long to experience, to meet, and to see. Others are drawn to verses stressing *jalal*, the majestic, awe-inspiring qualities of God. They conceive of their faith as a system of laws and regulations revealed by an omnipotent divine judge who is to be feared. Some conceive of the Quran as a recited text whose beauty is meant to evoke a transformative experience within the listener, while others conceptualize the Quran as primarily a political document, indeed a constitution, an essential prerequisite for the modern nation-state. Muslims have similarly invoked the figure of the Prophet Muhammad, who serves as a paradigm of faith, in conflicting ways. For instance, *hadith*s attributed to him have been cited both to liberate women from patriarchy as well as to subjugate them.

Given the challenge of saying anything intelligible about Islam in the face of the diversity of contradictory interpretations, I suggested in the introduction that the crucial questions we should ask are 'Which Islam?' 'Whose Islam?' 'In which context?' Asking these questions contextualizes the interpretation of religion and moves away from conceiving religious concepts as fixed things or objects. For example, the *shari'a*, which some Muslims and non-Muslims today regard as a set of immutable laws and regulations synonymous with and intrinsic to Islam, is not mentioned in the Quran even once. It is a concept that emerged 300 years after the death of the Prophet Muhammad from a set of fluid, evolving regulations deriving from the Quran, *hadith*, traditions of jurisprudence, and local custom. Since the multiple contexts in which religions are embedded are constantly changing, we should recognize that understandings of Islam are never static, but rather fluid and evolving. In this regard, Michael Muhammad Knight appropriately remarks in his book *Impossible Man*:

> I'd never claim to know what 'true' Islam stood for; religions were too big to make it that simple, there was too much history and too many verses, and everyone just took the parts that they wanted anyway. For a prophet's message to become what they call a world religion, it would have to be big enough to accommodate all kinds of personalities. Good ones, mean ones, greedy ones, kind

ones, hard ones, soft ones, and they all own
Islam as much as it owns them. The water has
no shape; it's shaped by the bottle.[1]

The essential element ('the water') that is
contained within these disparate shapes and
forms comprises certain concepts which have
been reified over time. These have been identified by various Muslim scholars as constituting
the theological core of Islam as a religion: belief
in divine unity and unicity (*tawhid*); the Quran
and the notion of revelation; the concept of
prophethood and the centrality of Muhammad
and his heirs as authoritative role models; belief
in the afterlife; and the associated notion of
accountability of human action.

Not surprisingly, even these core beliefs
which most Muslims hold in common are understood and interpreted across an incredibly wide
ideological spectrum. The Prophet Muhammad
is represented as a lawgiver, a mystic, an *avatara*,
a bridegroom, and a sage. Similarly, *tawhid* has
been understood in many ways, ranging from the
oneness of God to union with God and even
union with creation. To borrow another analogy
suggested by Barbara Petzen, these core concepts
form the basic ingredients of a recipe. Since these
ingredients can be cooked and seasoned (i.e.
interpreted) in different ways in accordance with
the tastes and predilections of the chef (i.e. the
interpreter), the result is many different recipes
each with their own flavour.[2] Or to use the analogy
of fabric, these core elements become unifying

threads across diverse cultures, interwoven with other cultural elements, such as the conception of Arabic as a sacred liturgical language, the prominence of Arabic calligraphy, the importance of poetic discourses transmitting the emotive knowledge of the heart, the transmission of traditionalism, and the institutionalization of authority. Talal Asad, a leading anthropologist of Muslim communities, has written about Islam in terms similar to what we have called a cultural studies approach. Asad speaks of Islam as a 'discursive tradition'. By this, he means that although most expressions of Islam share a set of conceptual, textual, and historical reference points, their meaning is continually renegotiated leading to a wide range of conceptions across time and space.[3]

Centring the Arts

In this book, we have emphasized the need to relate religion to the multiple dimensions in which it is embedded, including the emotive and the experiential. We have discussed the central role that the arts, broadly defined, play as the primary means through which Muslims across a broad spectrum of interpretations engage with their faith. Yet they have often been marginalized in narratives about Islam. Centring them permits us to address substantial gaps in our knowledge and understanding of Islam as a faith. Looking at religion as a multisensory phenomenon embedded in the arts provides an alternative to post-Enlightenment European notions of religion that are so prevalent around the world today and which have proven to be toxic, insofar as they have been instrumentalized by the discourses of colonialism and nationalism to divide and 'otherize' people based on their religion, sometimes with tragic consequences.

Although my experience of growing up Muslim involved a multisensory engagement with my faith, especially Quran recitations and devotional poetry, I did not, however, recognize the role of the arts in constructing and shaping knowledge about Islam until I came to Harvard and studied under Annemarie Schimmel. An extraordinary scholar who lived and travelled in many Muslim countries, she introduced me to the power of the arts, particularly poetry and calligraphy, which she saw as crucial to her own development as a scholar of Islam. The poetic arts in particular provided her with profound insights into the various cultures she studied and visited. As a result, she wholeheartedly embraced the perspective of the German philosopher Johann Herder (d. 1803) who wrote, 'From poetry we learn about eras and nations in much greater depth than through the deceitful and miserable ways of political and military war histories.'[4] During a speech she delivered at a March 1996 ceremony, where she was awarded the German Peace Prize for her achievements in generating understanding between East and West, Schimmel cited the importance of poetry in her own development as a scholar:

I have discovered Istanbul corner by corner through the verses which Turkish poets had sung for five centuries about this wonderful city; I have learned to love the culture of Pakistan through the songs that resound in all of its provinces, and when one of my Harvard students had the misfortune to be among the American hostages in Tehran, he experienced a great change in his jailers' attitude when he recited Persian poetry; here, suddenly, a common idiom emerged and helped to bridge deep ideological differences.[5]

The role that poetry can play in creating bridges of understanding in highly polarized contexts is not to be underestimated. In 1947, in the midst of communal riots and massacres unleashed by strident forms of religious nationalism that eventually led to the partition of the subcontinent, a train carrying Hindu and Sikh refugees fleeing riots in the city of Rawalpindi had stopped at the station of Arifwala in the Punjab on its way to the Indian border. Incited by hate-filled invective from some local *mullah*s, the mob was preparing to attack the train in revenge for Muslims who had been killed earlier by Hindus and Sikhs. Suddenly, the angry mob became quiet. A Sikh, apparently under the influence of opium, was hanging out of one of the windows of the train singing verses from one of the most famous epic poems of Punjabi literature, *Hir*. Composed between 1776 and 1777 in a village mosque by Varis Shah, a poet who has been called the Shakespeare of the Punjab, *Hir* is the most widely recited poetic version of the Punjab legend narrating the tragic and illicit love affair between Hir, the daughter of a local chieftain, and her beloved Ranjha, the son of a rival chieftain. The verses that the Sikh was singing were excerpts from the section of the epic in which the poet criticizes corrupt and hypocritical *mullah*s for denying Ranjha, the hero of the epic, hospitality in the mosque after he had fled from his family to be with Hir. Hearing these verses, the angry mob suddenly came to its senses and refused to obey the instruction of some *mullah*s to attack the train. Literally saved by verses of poetry, the train left the station unscathed. As Suba Singh, a witness, remarked, 'His eyes half-closed, the opium addict sang away and hatred turned into fellow feeling. Words were working a miracle. The soul of the Punjab was speaking through Varis Shah's soul.'[6] Clearly, Varis Shah's poetic rendition of the Hir–Ranjha romance expressed and symbolized, through its popularity, a fundamental ethic and ideal cultural unity shared by all Punjabis irrespective of their religious affiliation, a deep unity that had been forgotten in the zeal and passion of religious nationalism.

This incident provides a moving and dramatic testimony to the powerful role that poetic traditions can play in the daily lives of people, by resetting their worldviews. They can humanize that which has been dehumanized by some elites – political and religious. In this sense, they are not

merely sources of entertainment and vehicles
for transmitting heritage from one generation to
another; they are also forces promoting communal
harmony amongst peoples of different faiths by
creating shared understandings of what it means
to be human and providing common frameworks
for moral, ethical, and cultural discourses. They
also play a pivotal role in shaping multiple traditions of spirituality and mysticism. Unsurprisingly,
Varis Shah's *Hir*, notwithstanding its universal
appeal amongst all Punjabis, has been interpreted
within both the frameworks of Hindu Vedanta
philosophy as well as Islamic mysticism.

Final Thoughts

It is my hope that this book has demonstrated
that religions are far from static; they are fluid,
polyvalent, and inextricably embedded within
the evolving realities of people's lives. As these
realities shift, so too do the religious expressions
they inform. Although this book is ultimately
about a religious tradition – Islam – we have seen
time and again the dangers of fixating on religious
markers of identity to the exclusion of others.
Apart from impairing our ability to better understand the ways in which religious expressions are
constructed, this obsession with 'the religious'
often leads to structural violence. As Nobel Prize
winning economist Amartya Sen has noted:

> The world is made much more incendiary
> by the advocacy and popularity of single-
> dimensional categorization of human beings,

which combines haziness of vision with increased scope for the exploitation of that haze by the champions of violence.[7]

He brings to our attention that Muslims, like all human beings, have multiple identities, not simply their religious ones. These identities are not only intertwined with each other, but they also help connect individuals with people of other faiths and worldviews. Through these multiple identities we are connected to a broader mosaic of humanity which transcends the narrow boundaries imposed by religious ideologies. Viewing a person simply on the basis of their religious identity strips them of their humanity, inevitably leading to stereotypes and racism. On the other hand, privileging the voices of those in religious authority as being representative of all Muslims, as many states often do, can also be a mistake as it marginalizes all other voices. In this regard, Amartya Sen cautions:

> The confusion between the plural identities of Muslims and their Islamic identity is not only a descriptive mistake, it has serious implications for policies of peace in the precarious world in which we live . . . The effect of this religion-centered political approach, and of the institutional policies it has generated . . . has been to bolster and strengthen the voice of religious authorities while downgrading the importance of nonreligious institutions and movements.[8]

These comments resonate strongly with the cultural studies approach in this book, which has sought to include understandings of Islam from people with different perspectives, not only religious scholars. As we have seen in our exploration, we can learn as much about Islam from a poet as from a theologian.

Many exclusivist approaches, especially those that construct Islam as antithetical to everything Western, fly in the face of long-standing expressions of Islam which have much in common with traditions in the so-called West. We know that Western and Islamic traditions share many figures and concepts associated with the Abrahamic faiths and that both draw heavily on Greek thought, so we have to question the extent to which it is historically and intellectually justified to present these as different civilizations. Indeed, the historian Richard Bulliet has even proposed that it would be best to think about them as a single Islamo-Christian civilization.[9]

In examining the state of relationships between peoples from different nations, cultures, races, and religions in our increasingly fragmented world, we must be mindful of those intellectual and spiritual continuities that connect us, and not allow exclusivist strands of Islam or interpretations of the West to eclipse other more inclusivist forms and expressions of the tradition. Moreover, these continuities should lead us to seriously question the notion that has held currency both within Muslim communities and

Western contexts: the so-called clash of civilizations. Such rhetoric that supposes polarized
notions of 'Western' and 'Islamic' has been all
too common in recent years. In Europe, it often
manifests itself in xenophobic fears about Muslim
and non-European immigrants, whose cultural
backgrounds and practices are considered irre-
concilable with a European lifestyle. In an
American context, it has often taken on religious
and racial overtones which many use to emphasize the supposedly stark theological contrast
between Islam and Christianity. Here, too, these
fears are fuelled by a growing Muslim presence
in the United States, one that seems to challenge
the narrative of a monolithic and homogeneous
Christian nation. In Muslim-majority societies as
well, there are some groups and individuals who
have championed a binary world by emphasizing
the superiority of Islam and Muslims over other
cultures and faiths. In some cases, this has led to
a rhetoric of hate, and even violence. The issue,
then, is a pattern of mutual antagonism which
supposes that 'Islamic' and 'Western' are meaningful oppositional categories. Martha Nussbaum,
a noted American philosopher, has written
eloquently on this issue:

> The real 'clash of civilizations' is not the clash
> *between* 'Islam' and 'the West,' but, instead
> a clash *within* virtually all modern nations
> – between people who are prepared to live
> with others who are different, on terms of
> equal respect, and those who seek the protec-

tion of homogeneity, and the domination of a single 'pure' religious and ethnic tradition.[10]

In this regard, I have long advocated that the solution to cultural misunderstandings – the harmful consequences of which are all too apparent – will not be found in foreign policy, military intervention, or the securitization of the state. Only by learning to identify similarities with and respect differences between us and others and by creating inclusive societies will we truly be able to tackle the major issues of our time. For a multiethnic, multireligious, and multiracial world to function efficiently and peacefully, it is crucial that its citizens respect and understand their neighbours, different though they may be. For this to happen, we must pay greater attention to the need for greater cultural and religious literacy globally. Without it, peace will be undermined by suspicion and the fabric of societies torn asunder. The pronouncement of the Quran is clear:

O humankind, We have created you male and female, and made you into communities and tribes, so that you may know one another.

(Q. 49:13)

Glossary

Abbasids	A Sunni Muslim dynasty whose rule extended across the Middle East and Asia between 750 and 1258.
adhan	The Islamic call to prayer, proclaimed by a muezzin at the time of worship.
ahl al-kitab	Lit. 'people of the book'. This term refers to Jews, Christians, and Zoroastrians who, according to Islamic thought, have received a scripture (*kitab*) from God.
al-aqlam al-sitta	The six rounded, cursive scripts that are used in Arabic calligraphy. These six styles are *naskh*, *rihani*, *muhaqqaq*, *tawqi*, *riqa*, and *thuluth*.
arkan al-din	Lit. 'pillars of religion' (also called 'pillars of Islam'). This refers to the core obligations of Muslims. The number of pillars varies among Islamic groups.
aslama	Term meaning 'to submit or surrender oneself to God'.
asma al-husna	Lit. the 'beautiful names' of God. This refers to the 99 names describing God's attributes.
avatara	In Hinduism, this is the incarnation of a god or a goddess in human or animal form.

awliya sing. *wali*	Lit. 'friends'. The term refers to the spiritual friends of God, often prophets and saints, but more generally those who act in accordance with the principles of the Quran and the examples set by the Prophet.
baraka	Blessing bestowed by God upon people or objects.
batin	The inner or esoteric meaning of the Quran, achieved through the interpretation of its verses.
bhajan	South Asian devotional hymn sung as a mode of worship by Hindus.
caliph (or *khalifa*)	Title held by the successors of the Prophet. These were the political and religious rulers of various Muslim dynasties between 632 and 1924.
Dao	A fundamental concept in Chinese philosophy meaning the 'way' of the universe.
dargah	Tomb-shrine of a revered Muslim figure. Sometimes these also become pilgrimage sites.
dhammal	Ecstatic, whirling dance commonly performed in Sufi shrines in Pakistan.
dhikr	The remembrance of God through the recitation of specific formulas and prayers.
din	Commonly taken to mean 'religion', but in the Quranic sense and according to early Muslims it meant 'custom' or 'way of life'.

faqir A holy person or spiritual healer who has renounced worldly possessions to be closer to God, and to guide others on that path.

Fatimids An Ismaili Shi'i dynasty that ruled parts of North Africa and the Middle East between 909 and 1171.

ginan Devotional hymn of the Nizari Ismaili communities of South Asia.

hadith literature The body of collected sayings attributed to the Prophet Muhammad, as reported by his close companions and contemporaries.

hadith qudsi Lit. 'divine *hadith*'. These are the sayings of God but conveyed in the words of the Prophet.

hafiz al-Quran The title given in honour of someone who has memorized the entire text of the Quran.

hajj The pilgrimage to Mecca, which all Muslims are required to undertake at least once, if they are able.

huruf al-Quran Lit. 'letters of the Quran'. This was the Arabic script adapted to write almost all the languages of the Islamic world.

ibadat Acts of worship, such as prayer, fasting, and pilgrimage.

ihsan Meaning, 'to do things beautifully'. The highest dimension of faith believed to be achieved through a person's engagement with beauty.

ilham Divine or spiritual inspiration bestowed on spiritually elevated figures.

iman	Faith in God.
islam	Submission to God.
Ismailis	Adherents of a branch of Shi'i Islam that considers Isma'il, the eldest son of the Shi'i Imam Ja'far al-Sadiq (d. 765), as his successor.
jihad	Term which can mean spiritual struggle against vice, but also holy war.
jinn	Spirits which, in pre-Islamic Arabia, were thought to inspire poets' words with a powerful spiritual potency.
kafir	Infidel. One who rejects God.
khalifa	Successor to the Prophet Muhammad (see *caliph*).
khums	A type of almsgiving unique to Shi'i Muslims.
kiram al-katibin	Noble scribe angels thought to sit on a person's shoulder, writing down their every deed.
kirtan	Devotional hymn associated with Indian religious traditions.
kufic script	A type of Arabic script utilizing an angular style that originated in the city of Kufa.
al-lawh al-mahfuz	Lit. 'the Well Preserved Tablet'. This is the heavenly prototype of all earthly scriptures on which everything from eternity has been written.
mawlid	Commemoration of the Prophet's birthday, observed with prayer and festivities.
mi'raj	The Prophet's ascension to the highest heaven and his subsequent meeting with God.

muharram	An assembly attended by Shi'a to commemorate the martyrdom of Imam Husayn, the grandson of the Prophet Muhammad.
mu'min pl. *mu'minun*	A believer. One who has faith in God (see *iman*).
muslim	A person who submits to God (see *islam*).
qasida	A genre of poetry which arose in pre-Islamic times and which Muslim poets adapted for religious purposes.
qawwali	A uniquely South Asian genre of devotional music.
salat	Ritual prayer which all Muslims are required to perform.
sawm	The obligatory daylight fast during the month of Ramadan.
shahada	The Islamic creed of faith which states 'There is no god but God; Muhammad is the messenger of God'.
al-sirat al-mustaqim	Lit. 'the straight path'; an Islamic concept with parallels to the Dao in China. The similarities between the two facilitated the integration of Islam into China.
sunna	The customs and practices of the Prophet which Muslims seek to emulate.
tahara	Purity.
tawhid	Belief in divine unity and unicity.
ta'ziya	A form of drama, prevalent in Iran, commemorating the martyrdom of Imam Husayn.
Umayyads	The first Islamic dynasty. They ruled from 661 to 750.

umm al-kitab	Lit. 'Mother of the Book'. This is the heavenly prototype of all earthly scriptures on which everything from eternity has been written (see *al-lawh al-mahfuz*).
wahy	The divine inspiration bestowed on prophets.
walaya	In Shiʻi Islam, this is the obligatory devotion to the Imams and the family of the Prophet.
zakat	The obligation for all Muslims to give a portion of their income to charity.

Notes

Introduction

1 '"Islam" . . . became practically useful as a political boundary term, both to outsiders and to insiders who wished to draw lines around themselves.' Carl Ernst, *Following Muhammad: Rethinking Islam in the Contemporary World* (Chapel Hill, NC, 2003), p. 10.

2 For example, Sayyid Qutb (d. 1966) of the Muslim Brotherhood in Egypt and Abu'l-A'la al-Mawdudi (d. 1979) of the Jama'at-i Islami in Pakistan.

3 Ernst, *Following Muhammad*, p. 6.

4 Aga Khan IV, 'Signing of the Funding Agreement for the Global Centre for Pluralism' (speech, Ottawa, Canada, 25 October 2006). Transcript at https://the.akdn/en/resources-media/resources/speeches/signing-funding-agreement-global-centre-pluralism-ottawa.

5 Diane L. Moore, *Overcoming Religious Illiteracy: A Cultural Studies Approach to the Study of Religion in Secondary Education* (New York, 2007), p. 4.

6 Benazir Bhutto as quoted in Lois Fein, 'Rama Mehta Lecture: The Egalitarian Qur'an vs. Anti-feminist Interpretations', *The Second Century, Radcliffe News* [occasional newsletter] (June 1985), p. 1.

7 Moore, *Overcoming Religious Illiteracy*, p. 79.

8 Moore, *Overcoming Religious Illiteracy*, p. 79.

9 'Dekha Ibrahim Abdi: The Peace Maker', *Kitu Kizuri, Voice of the African Woman*, July–September 2008, p. 24.

10 See Chapters 2 and 3 of Wilfred Cantwell Smith, *The Meaning and End of Religion: A New Approach to the Religious Traditions of Mankind* (San Francisco, CA, 1978).

11 Ernst, *Following Muhammad*, p. 30.

12 Ernst, *Following Muhammad*, p. 51.

13 Mohammed Arkoun, 'Rethinking Islam Today', *Annals of the American Academy of Political and Social Science* 588 (2003), p. 38.

14 Arkoun, 'Rethinking Islam Today', p. 38.

15 Arkoun, 'Rethinking Islam Today', p. 19.

16 Paraphrased from Abdolkarim Soroush, taken from his interview in Farish Noor, *New Voices of Islam* (Leiden, 2002), pp. 15–16.

Chapter 1. Who is a Muslim?

1 Fred Donner, *Muhammad and the Believers: At the Origins of Islam* (Cambridge, MA, 2009), pp. 194–224.

2 Smith, *The Meaning and End of Religion*, p. 115. See also his chapter 'The Historical Development in Islam of the Concept of Islam as an Historical Development', in *Historians of the Middle East*, ed. Bernard Lewis and Peter Holt (London, 1962), pp. 484–502.

3 Ernst, *Following Muhammad*, p. 11.

4 Ahmet Karamustafa, 'Islam: A Civilizational Project in Progress', in *Progressive Muslims: On Justice, Gender and Pluralism*, ed. Omid Safi (Oxford, 2003), p. 104.

5 Arabic, like Hebrew, is a Semitic language. Most words in these languages are derived from roots usually consisting of three consonants. In Arabic, the verb '*aslama*' originates in the trilateral consonantal root *s-l-m*.

6 Johann Wolfgang von Goethe, *Diwan* (WA I, 6, 128) as cited in Shaykh Abdalqadir al-Murabit,

'Was Goethe a Muslim?', Way to Allah [website], http://www.way-to-allah.com/en/journey/goethe.html (accessed 27 January 2021).

7 *The Message of the Qur'an*, trans. and interpreted by Muhammad Asad (Gibraltar, 1984), p. 885, n. 17.

8 Smith, *The Meaning and End of Religion*, p. 103. As an example of an exclusivist reading of this verse, see the translation of the Noble Quran published by the Ministry of Islamic Affairs, Endowments, Dawa and Guidance of the Kingdom of Saudi Arabia.

9 Smith, *The Meaning and End of Religion*, p. 102.

10 For a detailed discussion of Muslim conceptions of *islam*, *iman*, and *kufr*, see Sachiko Murata and William Chittick, *The Vision of Islam* (St Paul, MN, 1994), pp. 37–42.

11 Annemarie Schimmel, *Mystical Dimensions of Islam* (Chapel Hill, NC, 1975), p. 254.

12 Murata and Chittick, *The Vision of Islam*, p. 41.

13 As quoted in Shafique Virani, *The Ismailis in the Middle Ages: A History of Survival, A Search for Salvation* (New York, 2007), p. vii.

14 'Rosary' is only one meaning of the word *tasbih*, which in its more general sense can also evoke 'glorification', especially of God.

15 Ali Asani, '"Oh That I Could Be a Bird and Fly, I Would Rush to the Beloved": Birds in Islamic Mystical Poetry', in *A Communion of Subjects: Animals in Religion, Science, and Ethics*, ed. Paul Waldau and Kimberley Patton (New York, 2006), p. 171.

16 Annemarie Schimmel, 'The Celestial Garden in Islam', in *The Islamic Garden*, ed. Elisabeth B. Macdougall and Richard Ettinghausen (Dumbarton Oaks, WA, 1976), p. 24.

17 For an extended discussion of the concept of the five pillars, see Natana Delong-Bas, *The Five Pillars of Islam* (Oxford, 2010).

18 Murata and Chittick, *The Vision of Islam*, p. xxv.

19 A. J. Wensinck, *The Muslim Creed: Its Genesis and Historical Development* (New York, 2008), pp. 26–27.

20 al-Qadi al-Nu'man, *Da'a'im al-Islam*, trans. Asaf Fyzee as *The Pillars of Islam, Volume 1*, revised and annotated by Ismail Poonawala (New Delhi, 2002), pp. 2–3.

21 *Shimmering Light: An Anthology of Ismaili Poetry*, trans. Faquir Muhammad Hunzai, intro. and ed. Kutub Kassam (London, 1996), pp. 72–73.

22 See the works of Marshall G. S. Hodgson, especially Chapter 4 of *Rethinking World History: Essays on Europe, Islam, and World History*, ed. Edmund Burke III (Cambridge, 1993).

23 Khaled Abou El Fadl, *The Great Theft: Wrestling Islam from the Extremists* (San Francisco, CA, 2005), p. 176.

24 Shahab Ahmed, *What is Islam? The Importance of Being Islamic* (Princeton, NJ, 2016).

25 Muhammad Iqbal, *Complaint and Answer (Shikwa and Jawab-i-shikwa)*, trans. A. J. Arberry (Lahore, 1961), p. 48.

Chapter 2. Following God's Beloved: Muhammad as the Ideal Muslim

1 Some portions of this chapter are drawn from my book *Celebrating Muhammad: Images of the Prophet in Popular Muslim Poetry* (Columbia, SC, 1995), co-authored with Kamal Abdel-Malek, in collaboration with Annemarie Schimmel.

2 Paraphrased from Muhammad Iqbal, *Asrar-i khudi* (Lahore, 1915), trans. Reynold A. Nicholson

(London, 1920; Project Gutenberg, 2018), lines 395–396, https://www.gutenberg.org/files/57317/57317-h/57317-h.htm.

3 Paraphrased from Iqbal, *Asrar-i khudi*, line 351.

4 Constance Padwick, *Muslim Devotions: A Study of Prayer-Manuals in Common Use* (London, 1961), p. 151.

5 Padwick, *Muslim Devotions*, p. 145.

6 R. Kevin Jacques, 'Fazlur Rahman: Prophecy, the Qur'an, and Islamic Reform', *Studies in Contemporary Islam* 4 (2002), p. 80.

7 This is my translation of an excerpt from the Urdu song 'Bekas pe karam kijiye'.

8 As cited in Annemarie Schimmel, *And Muhammad is His Messenger: The Veneration of the Prophet in Islamic Piety* (Chapel Hill, NC, 1985), p. 85.

9 Mervyn Hiskett, *A History of Hausa Islamic Verse* (London, 1975), p. 47.

10 Christiane Gruber and Frederick Colby, *The Prophet's Ascension: Cross-Cultural Encounters with the Islamic Mi'raj Tales* (Bloomington, IN, 2010).

11 Rumi, *Mathnawi*, 5:2738, as cited in *Rumi and Islam: Selections from His Stories, Poems and Discourses*, trans. and annot. Ibrahim Gamard (Woodstock, VT, [2012]), p. 133.

12 Rumi, *Mathnawi*, 1:1397, as cited in *Rumi and Islam*, p. 147.

13 This is a slightly amended version of Arthur J. Arberry's translation from *The Koran* (Oxford, 2008).

14 Suleyman Celebi, *Mevlid-i-Serif*, trans. Metin Mustafa, *'The Divine Comedy' of Suleyman Celebi and Mir Heidar: A Sufi Mystical Reading of Early Modern Turkic Representations of Prophet Muhammad's Isra and Mir'aj* (Sydney, 2022).

15 Hiskett, *A History of Hausa Islamic Verse*, p. 45.

16 Schimmel, *And Muhammad is His Messenger*, p. 190.

17 I use the term 'translated' here in the sense proposed by Tony Stewart who defines 'translation' as an interpretative strategy in which religious practitioners seek 'equivalence' among their counterparts. Tony Stewart, 'In Search of Equivalence: Conceiving the Muslim–Hindu Encounter Through Translation Theory', *India's Islamic Traditions, 711–1750*, ed. Richard Eaton (New Delhi, 2003), pp. 363–392.

18 Ayesha Irani, *The Muhammad Avatara: Salvation History, Translation, and the Making of Bengali Islam* (Oxford, 2020).

19 Ali Asani, 'In Praise of Muhammad: Sindhi and Urdu Poems', in *Religions of India in Practice*, ed. Donald S. Lopez, Jr. (Princeton, NJ, 1995), p. 166.

20 Muhammad Usiar Yang Huaizhong, 'The Four Upsurgences of Islamic Culture in Chinese History', *Journal of Muslim Minority Affairs* 16, no. 1 (1996), p. 9.

21 Historically, 'Hui' referred to Islam generally, and it is still often used in this way. Since the Republican period, however, and particularly since Communist rule, 'Hui' has increasingly come to designate this particular group of Muslims to distinguish them from Turkic Muslim groups.

22 Zvi Ben-Dor Benite, *The Dao of Muhammad: A Cultural History of Muslims in Late Imperial China* (Cambridge, MA, 2005), p. 164.

23 Ben-Dor Benite, *The Dao of Muhammad*, p. 3.

24 Ben-Dor Benite, *The Dao of Muhammad*, p. 170.

25 Ben-Dor Benite, *The Dao of Muhammad*, p. 175.

26 Ben-Dor Benite, *The Dao of Muhammad*, p. 168.

27 Ben-Dor Benite, *The Dao of Muhammad*, p. 176.

28 Ben-Dor Benite, *The Dao of Muhammad*, p. 180.

29 Ben-Dor Benite, *The Dao of Muhammad*, p. 192.

30 Verse by Persian poet Jami (d. 1492), as quoted in Schimmel, *And Muhammad is His Messenger*, p. 191.

31 Emel Esin, *Mecca the Blessed, Madinah the Radiant* (New York, 1963), p. 204.

32 Padwick, *Muslim Devotions*, p. 162.

33 Schimmel, *And Muhammad is His Messenger*, p. 304n. 74.

34 Abou El Fadl, *The Great Theft*, p. 54.

35 My translation of the quote taken from Ghulam al-Hasnain Panipati, *Safar-i Hajj, ya, Saman-i Akhirat* (Delhi, 1934), pp. 76–77.

36 Quoted in Schimmel, *And Muhammad is His Messenger*, p. 130.

37 Shakeel Badayuni as quoted in Schimmel, *And Muhammad is His Messenger*, p. 87.

Chapter 3. Multisensory Religion: Rethinking Islam

1 The quote is from Sir Sultan Muhammad Shah, Aga Khan III, excerpted from his interview with the *Daily Sketch*, 2 November 1931.

2 Arkoun, 'Rethinking Islam Today', p. 19.

3 See Alexandra Grieser, 'Aesthetics', in *Vocabulary for the Study of Religion*, ed. Robert Segal and Kocku von Stuckrad (Leiden, 2015), vol. 1, pp. 14–23.

4 See William Graham, *Divine Word and Prophetic Word in Early Islam* (Mouton, 1977).

5 Rudolf Otto, *The Idea of the Holy*, trans. John W. Harvey (Oxford, 1958).

6 Karen Armstrong, *Muhammad: A Biography of the Prophet* (San Francisco, CA, 1992), pp. 83–84.

7 Michael Sells, *Approaching the Qur'an: The Early Revelations* (Ashland, OR, 1999), p. 7.

8 Paraphrased from Q. 39:23.

9 Navid Kermani, *God is Beautiful: The Aesthetic Experience of the Quran*, trans. Tony Crawford (Cambridge, 2015), pp. 24–30.

10 Kermani, *God is Beautiful*, pp. 15–24.

11 Kermani, *God is Beautiful*, pp. 17–18. After the death of Muhammad, Umar became the second *khalifa/caliph* or 'successor'.

12 Kermani, *God is Beautiful*, pp. 35–37.

13 See, for example, Q. 17:88: 'If humans and Jinn banded together to produce the like of this *quran* [recitation] they would never produce its like even though they backed one another.' Also, Q. 52:33–34: 'Or do they say he has fabricated it? Nay! They believe not! Let them then produce a recitation like unto it if they speak the truth.'

14 Kermani, *God is Beautiful*, p. 25.

15 Oludamini Ogunnaike, 'The Silent Theology of Islamic Art', *Renovatio*, 5 December 2017, https://renovatio.zaytuna.edu/article/the-silent-theology-of-islamic-art (accessed 23 August 2023).

16 Kermani, *God is Beautiful*, p. 293.

17 Kristina Nelson, *The Art of Reciting the Qur'an* (Austin, TX, 1985), p. 191.

18 Kermani, *God is Beautiful*, p. 326.

19 Noura Durkee, 'Recited from the Heart', *Aramco World* 51, no. 3 (May/June 2000), https://archive.aramcoworld.com/issue/200003/recited.from.the.heart.htm (accessed 31 August 2023).

20 Darimi, *Sunan*, XXIII/33 (no. 3504), as cited in Kermani, *God is Beautiful*, p. 27.

21 Kermani, *God is Beautiful*, p. 141.

22 Durkee, 'Recited from the Heart'.

23 Durkee, 'Recited from the Heart'.

24 Sells, *Approaching the Qur'an*, p. 11.

25 Rudolph Ware, *The Walking Qur'an: Islamic Education, Embodied Knowledge, and History in West Africa* (Chapel Hill, NC, 2014).

26 Kristina Nelson, 'The Sound of the Divine in Daily Life', in *Everyday Life in the Muslim Middle East*, ed. Donna Lee Bowen and Evelyn Early (Bloomington, IN, 2002), pp. 260–261.

27 Mohammed Arkoun, 'The Notion of Revelation: From *Ahl al-Kitab* to the Societies of the Book', *Die Welt des Islams*, New Series, 28, no. 1/4 (1988), pp. 74–76.

28 Arkoun, 'The Notion of Revelation', p. 75.

29 'Calligraphy the Art of Making Words Sing', *UNESCO Courier* 5 (2009), pp. 7–8.

30 Annemarie Schimmel, *Calligraphy and Islamic Culture* (New York, 1984), pp. 77–78.

31 This is known as *sarnavisht* in Persian, *alın yazısı* in Turkish, *likha* in Urdu Hindi, and *likhyo* in Sindhi.

32 Schimmel, *Calligraphy and Islamic Culture*, p. 79.

33 The quote is taken from Schimmel, *Calligraphy and Islamic Culture*, p. 81.

34 Schimmel, *Calligraphy and Islamic Culture*, pp. 37–38.

35 Seyyed Hossein Nasr, *Islamic Art and Spirituality* (Albany, NY, 1987), p. 10.

36 Schimmel, *Calligraphy and Islamic Culture*, p. 23.

37 Michael Calabria, *The Language of the Taj Mahal: Islam, Prayer and the Religion of Shah Jahan* (London, 2022), pp. xii–xiv.

38 Calabria, *The Language of the Taj Mahal*, pp. xiii–xiv.

39 Muhammad Iqbal, *Javid-nama*, trans. A. J. Arberry (London, 1966), p. 45.

40 Sells, *Approaching the Qur'an*, p. 7.
41 Sells, *Approaching the Qur'an*, 11.
42 For more details on this legendary Muslim mystic, see Rkia Elaroui Cornell, *Rabi'a from Narrative to Myth* (La Vergne, 2019).
43 Rkia Elaroui Cornell, 'Rab'ia from Narrative to Myth: The Tropics of Identity of a Muslim Woman Saint' (PhD dissertation, Vrije Universiteit Amsterdam, 2013), p. 224.
44 Dawlatshah, *Tadhkirat al-shu'ara*, ed. Edward G. Browne (London, 1901), p. 197.
45 Patricia Almarcegui, 'Poetry and Memory: The Case of Iran', IEMed (European Institute of the Mediterranean) [website], https://www.iemed.org/publication/poetry-and-memory-the-case-of-iran/ (accessed 16 May 2025).
46 Nosheen Ali, 'Mannkahat: Poetic Knowledge and Shah Abdul Latif through Sur', paper presented at the 10th University of Michigan Pakistan Conference: Religious Landscapes, 2–3 April 2021.
47 Shemeem Burney Abbas, *The Female Voice in Sufi Ritual: Devotional Practices of Pakistan and India* (Austin, TX, 2002), p. 15.
48 Richard Burton, *Sindh, and the Races that Inhabit the Valley of the Indus* (London, 1851), p. 84.
49 Wendy M. K. Shaw, *What is 'Islamic' Art? Between Religion and Perception* (Cambridge, 2019), p. 28.

Conclusion

1 Michael Muhammad Knight, *Impossible Man* (New York, 2009), pp. 321–322.
2 Barbara Petzen is an educator and specialist in curriculum development. She has developed educational material on food as a tool for teaching

students about the geography, history, and politics of the Middle East.

3 See especially Talal Asad, 'The Idea of an Anthropology of Islam', *Qui Parle* 17, no. 2 (Spring/Summer 2009), pp. 1–30.

4 Quoted in Annemarie Schimmel, *Orient and Occident: My Life in East and West*, trans. Karen Mittmann (Lahore, 2007), p. 296.

5 Annemarie Schimmel, 'A Good Word is Like a Good Tree', Speech given at the German Book Trade's Peace Prize ceremony, March 1996, http://amaana.org/articles/schimtree.htm (accessed 2 March 2024).

6 Suba Sing, '*Varis-Shah-lok-kavi*', *Punjabi Dunia* 5, nos. 2–3 (1954), as cited in Jeevan Deol, 'Sex, Social Critique and the Female Figure in Premodern Punjabi Poetry: Varis Shah's *Hir*', *Modern Asian Studies* 36, no. 1 (2002), p. 141.

7 Amartya Sen, 'What Clash of Civilizations? Why Religious Identity is not Destiny', *Slate*, 29 March 2006, https://slate.com/news-and-politics/2006/03/what-clash-of-civilizations.html (accessed 11 April 2025).

8 Amartya Sen, *Identity and Violence: The Illusion of Destiny* (London, 2007), pp. 75 and 77.

9 Richard W. Bulliet, *The Case for Islamo-Christian Civilization* (New York, 2004).

10 Martha C. Nussbaum, 'The Clash Within: Democracy and the Hindu Right', in *Values and Violence: Intangible Aspects of Terrorism*, ed. Ibrahim A. Karawan, Wayne McCormack and Stephen E. Reynolds (Dordrecht, 2008), p. 83.

Select Reading List

Provided here is a list of readings to help the interested reader further enrich their knowledge of key aspects touched upon in this book.

Abou El Fadl, Khaled. *The Great Theft: Wrestling Islam from the Extremists*. San Francisco, CA, 2005.

Ahmed, Shahab. *What is Islam? The Importance of Being Islamic*. Princeton, NJ, 2016. (See also review articles by Frank Griffel, Michael Pregill, Wendy Shaw, and Milad Milani. Note that there is considerable overlap between the author's centring of poetry, Sufism, and art, and Shahab Ahmed's conceptualization of Islam as hermeneutical engagement with the text, pre-text, and context of revelation.)

Arberry, A.J., trans. *Discourses of Rumi*. London, 1961.

Arberry, A.J., trans. *The Koran Interpreted*. New York, 1955.

Griffel, Frank. 'Contradictions and Lots of Ambiguity: Two New Perspectives on Premodern (and Postclassical) Islamic Societies'. Review of *What is Islam? The Importance of Being Islamic*, by Shahab Ahmed. *Bustan: The Middle East Book Review* 8, no. 1 (2017), pp. 1–21.

Izutsu, Toshihiko. *Ethico-Religious Concepts in the Qur'an*. Toronto, 2002. (On the meaning of *kufr* and other terms.)

Kermani, Navid. *God is Beautiful: The Aesthetic Experience of the Quran*, trans. Tony Crawford. Cambridge, 2015.

Milani, Milad. 'Shahab Ahmed and the Hermeneutics

of Islam'. Review of *What is Islam? The Importance of Being Islamic*, by Shahab Ahmed. *Journal for the Academic Study of Religion* 33, no. 2 (2020), pp. 185–203.

Mottahedeh, Roy P. 'The Clash of Civilizations: An Islamicist's Critique'. *Harvard Middle Eastern and Islamic Review* 2, no. 2 (1995), pp. 1–26.

Nasr, Seyyed Hossein, editor-in-chief. *The Study Quran: A New Translation and Commentary*. New York, 2015. (For those seeking an authoritative accessible English version of the Qur'an, with commentary.)

Pregill, Michael. 'I Hear Islam Singing'. Review of *What Is Islam? The Importance of Being Islamic*, by Shahab Ahmed. *Harvard Theological Review* 110, no. 1 (2017), pp. 149–165.

Schimmel, Annemarie. *And Muhammad is His Messenger: The Veneration of the Prophet in Islamic Piety*. Chapel Hill, NC, 1985.

——. *Calligraphy and Islamic Culture*. New York, 1984.

——. *Mystical Dimensions of Islam*. Chapel Hill, NC, 1975. (A transnational treatment of Sufism.)

Schubel, Vernon. *Teaching Humanity: An Alternative Introduction to Islam*. New York, 2023.

Sells, Michael. *Approaching the Qur'an: The Early Revelations*. Ashland, OR, 1999. (This book also contains a CD of various styles of Qur'anic recitation.)

Shaw, Wendy. Review of *What is Islam? The Importance of Being Islamic*, by Shahab Ahmed. *Journal of Islamic Studies* 28, no. 3 (2017), pp. 378–382.

Smith, Margaret. *Rabiʿa The Mystic (A.D. 717–801)*. Cambridge, 1928.

List of Illustrations

Index

The letter *f* following an entry indicates a page with a figure.

World of Islam Series

The *World of Islam* series aims to provide non-specialist readers with a reliable and balanced overview of the diverse manifestations of Islam. It seeks to redress misperceptions by offering a nuanced survey of the plurality of interpretations amongst Muslims around the world and throughout history, who express their faith and values through varied cultural, social, intellectual and religious means. Covering themes pertinent to Muslims and non-Muslims alike, the civilizational series approach encourages readers to delve into the commonalities as well as the distinctions that define different Muslim traditions. In accessible language and concise format, these books deliver well-researched yet easy-to-follow introductions that will stimulate readers to think differently about Islam.

Be inspired by the World of Islam.

The Institute of Ismaili Studies

The Institute of Ismaili Studies, established in 1977, has an extensive programme of multilingual and interdisciplinary research and publications. Informed by rigorous scholarly research, we endeavour to make available texts relating to Islam and Muslim communities in their historical and contemporary contexts. Our focus is on Ismaili and related Shiʿi studies, Qurʾanic studies, and also Islam's diverse devotional, literary, intellectual, artistic, and esoteric traditions. Many of these publications highlight the relationship of faith and practice to broader dimensions of society, culture, and modern life.

Authors of the Institute's publications hail from various parts of the world and express a range of views and ideas, which are not necessarily those of the Institute itself.

A full list of the publications of the Institute of Ismaili Studies can be found on our website at www.iis.ac.uk.